★ ★ All About ★ ★
BAR·B·Q

KANSAS CITY - STYLE

Second Edition

RICH DAVIS & SHIFRA STEIN

Pig Out Publications, Inc.

ISBN 0-925175-11-0

Printed in the United States of America

Text and cover design: David Bugay
Cover photo: Rob Baker
Editor: Jane Doyle Guthrie

10 9 8 7 6 5 4 3 2 1 95 96 97 98 99

For corporate sales and special orders, or to receive a catalog, contact the publisher:

Pig Out Publications, Inc.
4245 Walnut Street
Kansas City, Missouri 64111
(816)531-3119
(816)531-6113 (fax)

★ ★ All About ★ ★
BAR·B·Q
KANSAS CITY - STYLE

★ CONTENTS ★

★ ACKNOWLEDGMENTS ★

No venture ever succeeds without the combined efforts of many people. We've been fortunate to find friends and allies whose input strengthened the production of this publication in 1995 for the second edition. Our sincere thanks go to the following:

Rob Baker for the cover photo;

Jane Guthrie for her eagle eyes;

David Bugay for our fresh new look;

Karen Adler for her encouragement and guidance;

Coleen Davis for gathering and sharing materials on barbecue from around the country; and

Our numerous family members and friends for their encouragement, constructive criticism, enthusiasm, and love.

★ FOREWORD ★

A handbook of just about everything you ever wanted or needed to know about barbecuing, especially à la The Heartland, *All About Bar-B-Q Kansas City–Style* offers a wealth of recipes and how-tos for making your own irresistible mouth-smearing creations. Ranging far beyond the expected brisket and ribs, the book includes recipes for fajitas, venison, lamb, chicken, trout, shrimp—even a whole pig! There are even a few tony numbers like smoked duck and turkey thrown in for good measure.

For apartment-dwellers who are personally barbecue-less, Rich Davis and Shifra Stein offer some mighty fine indoor cooking recipes as well, from barbecuing in your very own oven to those oh-so-necessary side dishes such as beans, potato salads, slaws, cornbread, and all that good stuff. And if you have any room left, the book tempts with some real down-home desserts like sweet potato pie (I personally can't wait to try Thunder Thighs' Indian Bread Pudding).

What this book really does is entice one to hop on the next plane to Kansas City for an orgy of barbecue and beer. Who knows? You might even run into Calvin Trillin at Arthur Bryant's.

Sue B. Huffman
Senior Vice President, Programming
Television Food Network

★ PREFACE ★

Take fresh, thin slices of slowly smoked barbecued beef brisket, pile them high on a cushion of plain white bread, and slather with thick, brick-red barbecue sauce. Top with another slice of bread and hickory-smoked ham, and crown with more spicy sauce, dill pickles, and another slice of bread. This, friends, is barbecue, Kansas City–style. What Carnegie Deli's classic Reuben is to New York, this 4-inch-high sandwich is to Kansas City—along with everything else from juicy baby back ribs to succulent smoked trout.

Some of the best barbecue restaurants anywhere on earth can be found in Kansas City. Slabs of ribs, brisket, lamb, sausage, and fresh-cut, unpeeled fries cooked in lard are the hallmarks of this culinary art. Every joint also carries its favorite style of native Kansas City barbecue sauce, guaranteed to bring jaded taste buds back to life. Here wonderworks of the area's pitmasters are served in an atmosphere as warm and vital as the food itself.

Barbecue has become such a hot item in Kansas City that its popularity has spilled over past the confines of restaurants into homes and outdoor barbecue competitions. The Kansas City Barbeque Society has become a formidable-sized organization with well over 1,000 members. The members' aim is to promote great barbecue and to have fun while doing so. The society sanctions barbecue contests throughout the country and promotes fair rules for judging contests. In Kansas City, annual barbecue contests have brought out the best to compete in championship cook-offs on a par with those of Texas, Tennessee, Kentucky, and the Carolinas.

Current Kansas City barbecue contests run the calendar almost every weekend from spring until fall. Most noteworthy is the American Royal/K.C. Masterpiece International Invitational Barbecue Contest, which hosts a by-invitation-only event as well as an open-to-the-public competition and the International Barbecue Sauce Contest. (Many of the winners of area contests have their recipes highlighted in this book.)

There is so much to the mystique and mastery of this food that we can hardly contain it all within the pages of this one book. What we've tried to do is offer readers a tempting sampling of the many fine restaurants, recipes, and resources the Heartland has to offer. *Bone* appétit!

★ THE ORIGINS OF KANSAS CITY BARBECUE ★

Where lies the beginning of Kansas City–style barbecue? The answer probably rests somewhere in the roots of inner-city barbecue restaurants, which became, from the 1920s on, a melting pot of sauces and traditions brought north to this river town from the heart of Texas and the open-pit grills of the Deep South. This background is most likely responsible for Kansas City's famous barbecue sauces.

Fine-tuned with the individual barbecuing techniques acquired on Midwestern soil, Kansas City–style barbecue has emerged as a unique yet eclectic food. It is not restricted to the whole-hog pork of the Carolinas, the famous barbecued beef brisket of Texas, or the barbecued ribs of Memphis. Kansas City has its own favorites, and when it comes to flavor and quality, it can match the best.

GETTING THE WORD OUT

It took a Kansas Citian to tell the world that barbecue was, indeed, alive and well in the Heartland. When renowned author and columnist Calvin Trillin left his hometown for the Big Apple, he left part of his heart behind at Bryant's Barbecue at 18th and Brooklyn. Over the years Trillin has penned books and magazine stories about his one great love. America finally got his message, and Kansas City was thrust into the national limelight as a barbecue mecca—after having existed as one long before Trillin exposed the secret. What most people outside the city don't know is that Bryant's is only one of over 90 barbecue restaurants in town!

Barbecue has made missionaries out of visitors and fanatics out of residents, some of whom can't go a week without a fix of smoky, tangy ribs. Some of the urban joints have moved to classier neighborhoods, attracting a new clientele to an old way of cooking. But there are purists who would never go into a barbecue restaurant that reeks with cleanliness. They squirm at being served by waitresses in coordinated outfits and listening to Muzak with each bite.

The truth is, though, that Formica and grease do not necessarily make great barbecue greater. One should be broad-minded when in search of culinary genius. Some good barbecue does exist in new establishments, just as poor barbecue occasionally gets dished up in a "hole-in-the-wall." The evolution of KC 'que has offered diners many delicious options over the years.

HENRY PERRY

Kansas City barbecue didn't really start with Charlie and Arthur Bryant. The phenomenon began back in the late '20s, with a long, lean fellow called

Henry Perry. At the beginning of the Depression, Perry moved inside a street-car barn at 19th and Highland and started barbecuing in an outdoor pit. He served up slabs of barbecued ribs wrapped in newspaper to make ends meet.

Reputed to be "the father of barbecue" in Kansas City, Perry passed on his style and technique, influencing men such as Charlie and Arthur Bryant, George Gates, and Otis Boyd—each of whom eventually stamped his own brand of barbecue on beef and ribs. This legacy of Henry Perry has now become a Kansas City tradition that must be experienced to be understood. And it is this style that makes Kansas City barbecue an experience to be savored.

ARTHUR AND CHARLIE BRYANT

In March of 1981, the world's most famous chefs had arrived in New York to dine on America's best food and wine. From all around the country came cuisine to startle the taste buds: gumbo and red snapper bathed in Creole sauce, Tex-Mex salsa, key lime pie, and much, much more. What was Kansas City's contribution? Ribs from the renowned Bryant's Barbecue.

How Bryant's ribs made it to the forefront of American cuisine is an interesting story. Arthur Bryant was reared on an East Texas farm. The son of poor farmers, he migrated from there to earn a degree in agriculture in a town called Prairie View. He had the promise of a job in Amarillo, but he never made it. In 1931 he stopped in Kansas City to see his brother Charlie, who was working at "Old Man Perry's" place on 19th Street. Perry offered Arthur a job and Arthur stayed. That was the beginning.

Arthur often spoke with reverence about Charlie and Henry being the "great ones" in the business, the ones who taught him all he knew. Many will agree that Perry and the Bryant brothers were a triumvirate of the finest barbecue men who ever lived.

When Perry died, Charlie took over the business, and when Charlie retired in 1946, Arthur bought the restaurant and made some cosmetic changes, replacing wooden tabletops with Formica and putting down linoleum floors instead of sawdust. Later he even installed air conditioning. He never placed much emphasis on decor, though, saying that "you can't get too fancy, or you get away from what the place is all about."

The one major change he made was the sauce. Arthur once said of Perry that, while he taught him the essentials of good barbecue, his mentor was one "mean outfit." Perry, according to Bryant, enjoyed watching customers gasp as they gulped down water after their first taste of his sauce, which supposedly was one of the hottest ever made. Arthur wanted to make it "a pleasure" for people to savor his sauce. Having once hinted that his sauce contained paprika, red pepper, salt, and tomato puree rather than ketchup, Bryant settled on a moderately spicy recipe that has lasted to this day.

When Charlie died in 1952, Arthur felt that leaving the business was responsible for his brother's death. So Arthur stayed on, first operating out of his building at 18th and Euclid, then later at the present location at 18th and Brooklyn, preparing barbecue from early morning to late at night. There were times he wanted to give it up but, like the barbecue itself, the work was addictive.

The only respite he allowed himself came during the month of January, when he gave his employees a month's paid vacation and he took a rest, too. Then it was back to the pits, cooking up at least 2,000 pounds of U.S. Choice briskets a day.

The beer Arthur served became almost as famous as the beef. Frosty glass mugs stowed in a deep freeze enhanced the flavor of the brew. As do Bryant's famous, unpeeled fries—still cooked today in lard and sizzled in fat at 400 degrees Fahrenheit.

In the past, sensitive newcomers to the restaurant were occasionally shocked by the same grime and grease that Calvin Trillin found so endearing. And only occasionally were the countermen awed enough to use tongs to handle the meat, such as the time back in 1937 when Emperor Haile Selassie of Ethiopia made a visit. But, as many aficionados claim, the taste of the ribs is partly the counterman's hand anyway.

Bryant developed what he termed a "bum ticker" in his later years, and in 1982 it claimed his life. There was widespread sorrow and sadness at the passage of this legendary Kansas Citian. The restaurant continues to operate from the building that is a shrine to the formidable "king" of Kansas City barbecue.

GEORGE AND OLLIE GATES

Kansas City barbecue is also synonymous with Ollie Gates and his father, George, who also was influenced by Old Man Perry. George Gates made barbecue his life, starting out in 1945 when he began experimenting with different sauces. In 1949 he found the right recipe and it's been the same ever since, with some new flavors added along the way.

George W. Gates and a partner bought O'Johnny's O' Kentuck Bar-B-Q at 19th and Vine in 1946. Gates later bought out his partner and eventually moved to 24th and Brooklyn, doing business as Gates Ole Kentuck Bar-B-Q. His son, Ollie, began working at the restaurant as a teenager. Eventually Gates moved to a new location on 12th and Brooklyn. In 1958 Ollie Gates left his dad's business to start up his own restaurant.

Ollie Gates stands six feet three and could pass for a football player, but his expertise is in the field of barbecue. Since he started his operation, Gates Bar-B-Q has expanded to include several restaurants in various locations around the city. His "Rib Tech" school trains his pitmasters. Like Hertz and Avis, Gates and Bryant's draw their own devoted admirers who swear that one place is better than the other. The truth, of course, is totally subjective.

OTIS BOYD

Otis Boyd claims to be the only "complete barbecue man still living in Kansas City," having taken his formal training at a chef's school in Chicago in 1939. "Don't know anybody else cooking barbecue today that can say that," Boyd states simply.

How he has remained one of Kansas City's unsung heroes of barbecue is a mystery. He's had loyal fans as far back as the mid-'40s, when he opened his home-style restaurant at the historic corner of 12th Street and Vine—the heart of Kansas City jazz history.

Boyd's experience shows in the excellent product he turns out from the grease-encrusted aromatic pit that forms one wall of his kitchen at 55th and Prospect. The fragrant hickory smoke fills the room when the pit's big steel doors open. That odor has been a part of Boyd's life for nearly 40 years.

An amiable man, Otis Boyd is a walking oral barbecue historian who recalls that when he arrived in Kansas City in 1942, barbecue was still largely confined to urban areas with a large black population. "Sometime after World War II barbecue began to catch on in the suburbs, too," Boyd says, "especially when people started using backyard grills."

Boyd learned to blend spices for his barbecue sauce from "whatever was around the kitchen." In addition, he takes pride in making his own sausage, which many claim is the best in town.

NEW LEGENDS AND ENTREPRENEURS

Modern-day barbecue legends Hayward Spears, Jack Fiorella, and Rich Davis have added their successful restaurants and barbecue style to the Kansas City scenario with Hayward's Pit Bar-B-Que, Smoke Stack Bar-B-Q of Martin City, and K.C. Masterpiece Barbecue & Grill, respectively, as have so many others that we've listed them in the back of this book. The family-owned tradition among these restaurant dynasties is strong and promises to continue the bar-becue heritage in Kansas City. Potential success stories also abound among the growing number of 90–plus restaurant operations in this city. Add to that the entrepreneurs with barbecue-related businesses, ranging from sauce and spice companies and retail shops, to wood purveyors, grill and smoker manu-facturers, and you've got All About Bar-B-Q Kansas City–Style!

★ TOOLS, TIPS, AND TECHNIQUES ★

Nearly every rule about barbecuing springs from ordinary common sense. The supposed secrets and "mystique" about great barbecue make people somewhat fearful of approaching outdoor cooking. So here's a chance for everyone to get in on the fun. It's not hard at all—just a little messy, perhaps.

GRILLING VERSUS BARBECUING

In Newark, New Jersey, a misguided young man invited dinner guests to a backyard "barbecue," serving them charred steaks cooked over an open flame. When that same man moved to Kansas City, he learned that he'd committed a common error by referring to grilled foods as barbecued. "I always thought barbecue meant cooking steaks on the grill," he admitted. "When I came to Kansas City, I found out differently."

He wasn't alone in his delusion. There are many who confuse barbecuing and grilling, thinking that cooking hamburgers on a hibachi is barbecuing. There is a distinct difference between the two techniques. Grilling is done quickly, and the meat is seared fast to maximize juice retention. Steaks, chops, hamburgers, fish, and marinated chicken work well for this method. High, direct heat produces fast results, sealing in moisture and cooking the food quickly before it toughens. Grilling is like frying or sautéing; barbecuing is similar to roasting.

BARBECUING VERSUS SMOKING

The Chinese method of "cold smoking" various meats is excellent, but it isn't barbecuing. Cold smoking is related to the native American Indian way of preserving meats—the same methods used today by the smokehouses of Virginia. The fire, coals, or wood burn at a distance from the meats, which are hung on open racks, so that the smoke does not cook the meat.

Such meats can be smoked many hours, often hanging for more than a day in the cold smoker. (Some old-time methods called for three weeks of smoking.) If these meats were used immediately, they would be inadequately cooked and tough; the majority must be baked in the oven or cooked additionally in some way, with salt-cured foods soaked in water first.

Barbecued foods, on the other hand, are both smoked and cooked. Adhering to the following principles is important if you want to make the most of your time and money when you prepare genuine Kansas City barbecue. Barbecuing Kansas City–style is like learning how to drive a car. Once you've got the basics, the rest is easy.

BARBECUE UNITS

To begin with you'll need the right type of equipment and a knowledge of the varieties of grills you can use. By reading the manufacturer's directions, you'll learn how to maneuver the air vents, adjustable grids, fire pans, and covers.

Barbecue rigs range from gas grills, hooded braziers, and square-covered cookers to water smokers, portable grills, and kettle cookers—not to mention the homemade varieties. If you aren't a do-it-yourselfer, you can choose from brands such as Kingsford, Hasty Bake, Weber, Oklahoma Joe, and others. The right unit depends upon your lifestyle and the type of cooking you plan to do.

The *open brazier* is really nothing more than a shallow metal pan with a grid on top. Some braziers have half-hoods, covers, or battery-operated rotisseries. Tabletop hibachis are also considered open braziers. These are perfect for grilling hamburgers, steaks, poultry, and fish, but are not suited for serious slow smoking.

Covered cookers come in all shapes and are quite versatile. When you take the cover off, the smoker acts as a grill. These types of cookers have adjustable fire pans or grids, and vented covers for controlling heat. With dampers to control fire temperature, you can cook larger pieces of meat. When these cookers are covered, they can be used to barbecue.

While covered cookers usually come with a thermometer in the lid, these gauges aren't always dependable. It's better to have a regular meat or grill-top thermometer to avoid mistakes. You can also adjust the distance between the food and coals by raising or lowering the fire grate. Some models also have a fire door that allows you to add more fuel without opening the top.

Expensive wagon models are usually made of heavy metal with a heat-resistant finish. You can buy accessories for these, including rotisseries, extra grills, and smoking equipment.

The *Kamado oven* is ceramic and looks like a big egg, with the small end flattened to make it stand upright. It boasts a controllable smoke vent and draft door. The top third acts as a lid. When the lid is open, you can grill; closed, the smoker becomes an excellent oven.

A firebox at the bottom has an iron grate to contain the charcoal. You can barbecue with charcoal alone or use hardwood chips in addition. There is a Chinese oven similar to the Kamado, but it's barrel-shaped rather than looking like an egg. Both have inspired people who want to make their own ovens, using the pull-out firebox technique that makes it easy to add charcoal in small amounts throughout the cooking process.

Water smokers have a heavy, dome-shaped top and a built-in water pan. Many outdoor enthusiasts use these for cooking game and fish. You can slow-cook your food in these ovens, flavoring them with your favorite woods and letting the meat automatically baste and bathe in the moisture. Some serious barbecuers don't like this method because the meat is permeated by the water and doesn't get the hard, crusty finish it does with dry smoking.

The idea of *gas grills* might insult traditionalists who rail at the idea of smoking without charcoal, but these units are quite popular and more economical to operate than charcoal barbecues. They also are ready to use in a short time and cleaning is a breeze. However, be sure your gas grill is capable of producing the low temperature settings necessary for slow cooking. There are adjustable gas grills on which you can shut off the heat to one side to allow for a cooler area to barbecue food, leaving the heat source on the opposite side. However, the fire source and the grill are usually at a fixed distance from each other.

The actual taste you get from cooking with gas comes from the flavor of the smoke produced by the fat dripping onto the volcanic lava rock. You can also sprinkle water-soaked hickory chips or sawdust on the rocks to enhance the flavor if the manufacturer's directions permit. (Don't cover the gas outlet holes.) Whether or not this is barbecue depends on your definition of the subject—nothing duplicates the flavor of hardwood charcoal.

If you're in Kansas City long, you'll also encounter *homemade smokers.* There are those inventive and intrepid enthusiasts who much prefer to make their own smoke ovens. In Kansas City everything from barrels to electric cookstoves and cement blocks are in constant use in people's backyards and at barbecue contests. If you are serious about the subject, you might want to investigate making your own. While we can't give you all the instructions in the limited space of this book, we can recommend you attend some national or regional barbecue contests where these types of smokers are in use. Some contestants offer their homemade devices for sale; others sell instruction kits.

There are several requirements to building an efficient smoke oven: a fire pan to create heat and smoke; an area to confine the smoke; racks or hooks to hold the meat; an adequate draft and controllable air inlet near the source of the smoke; and air outlets at the top of the smoker, if possible. The illustrations on p. xx show several versions of the "perfect" smoker.

ACCESSORIES

To produce good barbecue, you'll need the right accessories. It's essential that you have tools that are easy to clean and handle. A utensil rack on the grill keeps them nearby.

Thermometers. A meat thermometer comes in handy for large cuts of meat that may not get done on the inside without some sort of meat probe. An oven thermometer gauges oven temperature. A grill thermometer is made to place on the rack of the grill for registering internal grill temperature

Tongs. You'll need two sets of tongs: one for coals, the other for food.

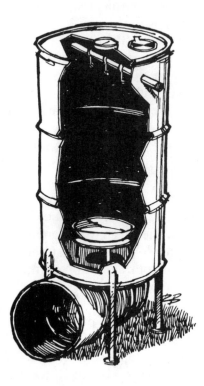

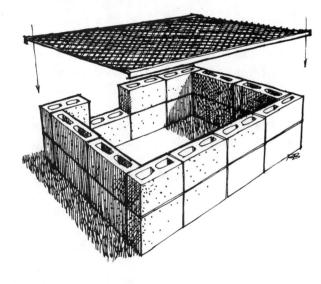

AL BOHNERT'S PIG PIT

A smoker oven can easily be made of standard cement blocks using a level, firm foundation. No mortar is necessary since the pit is designed to be semi-permanent. Bohnert's grand pit is designed to feed people who tend to make hogs of themselves. It's the one he's used when competing at barbecue contests.

PAUL KIRK'S "THE PIG"

This variation using a chemical-free 55-gallon drum can smoke 22 slabs of pork ribs or 90 pounds of brisket at one time. The pig smoker may be purchased fully assembled with instructions and recipes. You can also get easy-to-follow plans to build it yourself.

LINDSAY SHANNON'S SUPER SMOKER

Barbecue restaurateur Lindsay Shannon built his smoker from a 55-gallon drum and turned it horizontally, using bicycle handle bars to maneuver it.

Long-handled metal spatula and fork. The spatula turns the food and the fork spears the veggies (but don't pierce the meat, or the juices will flow into the charcoal instead of your mouth).

Long-handled basting brush or mops. Brushes or mops are used to baste the sauce on the meat during cooking.

Gloves, mitts, or hot pads. These should be heavy duty and able to withstand high temperatures. It's preferable to use extra-long mitts for handling hot grills and avoiding splatters.

Spray bottle for water and baking soda. Keep these close at hand to extinguish inevitable flare-ups.

Charcoal starters. Choose either the electric, liquid, or chimney type, as you like.

Hinged grill baskets. These contraptions are ideal for turning foods such as fish, hamburgers, or pork chops.

Long-handled skewers. These are perfect for kabobs. The flat metal kind are preferable so that cubed food doesn't spin when you turn it over.

Grill topper. Invest in one or more of these for fish and small items that might fall through the grill.

STARTING A PROPER FIRE

Knowing the number of ways and products available to start an outdoor fire for barbecuing goes along with learning the principles of good barbecue. Here are several methods:

Newspapers and kindling. One of the most common and simplest ways to start your barbecue is the way people have started fires in their fireplaces for generations. Twist some newspapers into long log-like links. Make two crossed layers of wadded-up newspapers. On top of them, place small pieces of twigs for dry kindling. For hardwood-cooking fires in big pits, use small logs, or add charcoal briquets on top of the kindling in order to ignite the charcoal. Light the edges of the newspapers on all sides. If the fire has been built properly, before long the charcoal will begin to get white.

One disadvantage of this type of fire is that unless it is built with a slight indentation in the middle of the newspaper-kindling area, the charcoal will scatter about the cooking unit as the paper and twigs eventually burn away. This is why this method is a less effective way to start your fire than some of the others described.

Electric fire-starters. A simple way to start a fire is by using an electric fire-starter. Place it in the center of your cooker, and pile the briquets on top according to the manufacturer's directions. When the briquets begin to turn red (around 10 or 20 minutes, depending upon the unit and the outdoor temperature), you can turn off the electrical apparatus and remove it when cool.

The major hazard here is forgetting about the unit and having it get too hot, thereby damaging it or the oven. Inserting a timer between the electrical outlet and the plug for the starter probably is a good idea. Set the timer according to the instructions on the electrical starter.

Each electrical fire starter should have its own instructions you should carefully follow. Caution: These units remain very hot for some time after unplugging, so set yours in a safe place while it's cooling off.

Liquid fire-starters. Never use kerosene, gasoline, or quick-igniting fuels when starting a barbecue fire. Instead, start your fire by stacking 12 to 20 briquets in a pyramid in the center of the cooker, then spray on a liquid fire-starter specifically designed for barbecuing. These commercial preparations have a much lower flashpoint and are much safer.

The disadvantage of this method is the lingering odor that can attach itself to the food. If the meat is put on before the charcoal ashes down, chemical fumes can ruin the flavor. The fire also can go out if you don't use enough starter fuel.

Never try to restart a fire that already has been lit by dousing the coals with more fuel. This is dangerous, as there still may be live coals that can flare up and burn you. Liquid fire-starters are meant to be used on charcoal before it is ignited. Use plenty the first time!

Fuel-coated substances. These materials range from fuel-soaked barbecue briquets to wood products or sawdust compressed into sticks that include an igniter fluid. These fire-starters can be inserted in the middle of the cooker and the briquets piled on top. You light a match to these and with adequate ventilation they catch fire and burn long enough to ignite the charcoal before burning themselves out. Again, fumes and odors can result from this method, unless the chemicals burn down completely before food is placed on the grill. Sometimes coated products don't catch on fire as easily as liquid fire-starters, particularly if they are old or have been left uncovered for a while. However, they are the easiest to use and the least trouble of any charcoal product.

Thick, jelly fire-starters. These substances are considered safer than liquid fire-starters, although they have never been quite as popular for some reason. Simply spread the jelly over your charcoal and light.

Metal "chimney" fire-starters. This is probably the best, safest, and cheapest method of all. The "chimney" is simply a round piece of metal about 6 to 12 inches in diameter and 8 to 15 inches high, much like a large tin can with both its bottom and top removed. A chimney fire-starter has the advantage of never having a chemical odor or taste to impart to the food. There is also no cost of fuel source, other than charcoal.

A lattice-like insert toward the bottom of this unit holds charcoal in the upper portion. Below this, you insert crinkled newspaper to serve as your fire source. Punctured holes around the bottom allow ventilation as the newspaper burns and ignites the charcoal above. Once the coals are reddish in color, they can be dumped out into the barbecue unit.

Make sure your unit has enough space to enable you to utilize the chimney effectively. One disadvantage here is that there is usually a handle on this device for charcoal removal. The handle can become quite hot, so either buy one that's insulated or wear gloves.

Butane, natural gas, and electric outdoor grills. These cookers can be lit automatically or with a match, and the heat source becomes available instantly— the advantages are obvious. There are those who prefer these types of grills simply because little clean-up is necessary and no chemical starters are needed. However, these grills lack the natural flavorings that come from hardwood charcoal and soaked chips. Some manufacturers say that you can add soaked chips to their units to help the taste, but be sure to check first, since ashes can plug up the tiny gas vents.

True barbecue pros shun such artificial devices. There are heated arguments among some professional restaurant barbecuers as to whether it is genuine barbecue if one even uses gas only to ignite hickory or oak logs—really!

In general, starting a barbecue fire with a source of heat intense enough to ignite the charcoal briquets is a simple procedure. Follow the instructions carefully for each method discussed and you'll be able to start a fire safely. Ordinary precautions about where the fire is built, how far away it is from the house, and whether or not there are small children or pets nearby are certainly necessary considerations when barbecuing outdoors.

It also makes sense to avoid firing up the grill near valuable shrubbery or underneath a low-limbed tree. Just look around you and be sure you've done everything necessary to ensure your barbecue turns out to be fun and enjoyable. Exercise good old common sense, and you should have no problems at all.

If you have a flare-up, don't panic. This usually indicates your fire is too hot for closed-pit barbecuing. It could also mean that the meat is directly over the briquets and dripping fat into the fire. Be sure to have a ready means of dousing the flames fast without reducing the heat. A plastic plant sprayer filled with water works well in emergencies. Be careful to spray the water on gently so it won't shower the meat with ashes.

USING THE RIGHT WOODS

There are many varieties of woods used for grilling and smoking meats. Since we are talking primarily about barbecuing and not grilling, we'll discuss woods commonly used in Kansas City–style barbecue. But first it's important to know what different sizes of woods can do.

There is a distinct difference in the utilization of wood products for barbecuing. Hickory and other woods in the form of *sawdust or small chips* burn fast when placed on the grill, so it's important to soak them in water for at least 30 minutes before using. This cut of hardwood provides immediate results, imparting a light, smoky flavor that enhances a quickly seared steak or other food that doesn't need cooking for a long period of time. These fine particles of wood are used for grilling, not true barbecuing.

In barbecuing, when you need smoke produced over several hours, you'll want *larger chunks or even small pieces of wood logs* that have been soaked in water for several hours. Many barbecuers advise letting the largest chunks soak at least 24 hours, so choose your size depending on purpose, just as you need to select varieties of woods for their particular flavors.

Hickory. Hickory is probably one of the most popular woods in the United States for barbecuing. It's available in diverse sections of the country and is also an excellent hardwood that burns slower than the softer woods to produce an excellent smoke flavor. However, too-heavy a hickory smoke over a long period tends to turn foods bitter. This is also true of mesquite.

Hickory wood is fine for smoking meat from turkeys to brisket, pork, and goat. Of all the varieties of hickory, shaggy bark hickory gives the sweetest smoke flavor. If you're lucky enough to live in an area where hickory is a native wood, you can even build your fire using small hickory logs. Just make sure your cooker can be closed down enough so that you're mostly heat smoking rather than cooking with live fire. Live fire hickory, of course, is excellent for grilling any kind of meat that needs to be seared and cooked quickly.

Mesquite. This wood has been around forever in the Southwest and has increased in popularity nationwide. One of the hardest woods known, mesquite produces a distinct, smoky flavor. Mesquite charcoal produces the high temperatures necessary for searing meats and sealing the juices inside, and thus is better for grilling than barbecuing.

The flavor of mesquite, like hickory, can become bitter if you smoke it over the fire for too long. However, barbecued brisket has been cooked as long as 20 hours using mesquite, with delicious results. It all depends on the control used to vary the amount of smoke and temperature, as well as the preparation of the foods to be smoked.

The cooking temperature for mesquite is often as high as 900 to 1,000 degrees Fahrenheit or more. The mesquite charcoal is rather smoky and has a habit of popping little fine sprays of red sparks as it continues to heat. If you're using mesquite for the first time, don't worry about this phenomenon. It isn't a sign of an inferior product—just of good mesquite charcoal.

Fruitwoods. Most of the common fruitwoods are considered excellent for barbecuing. The most popular and easily available are apple, cherry, peach, and pear. Lately grapevines and clippings have also been used. Cherry has a good flavor when mixed with other woods, although it's generally less available than most. If you're lucky enough to have a contact at a local fruit orchard, you might ask if, after the trees are pruned, you could keep the clippings, which are excellent sources of smoke.

Smaller clippings can be tossed on the grill when cooking hamburgers or steaks. Soak the larger chunks in water and use them in straight barbecuing.

Maple and corncobs. This combination is commonly used in the Northeastern part of the United States, where folks have easy access to both components. The excellent flavor this duo produces has been imparted to some of the famous hams and Canadian bacon that come out of Vermont.

Alderwood. This is a superior wood for smoking, famous for the alder-smoked salmon of the Northwest.

Sassafras and sassafras root. The good news is that sassafras is probably the best flavoring wood to use for smoking; the bad news is that it's hard to obtain. In addition, certain chemicals contained in sassafras tea are considered health hazards, although no specific studies we know of have been done on the smoking of foods with sassafras wood or root.

Over the years, one Southern Missouri family-owned smokehouse has produced fine prize-winning bacons and hams smoked with this exotic root. Plenty of folks have consumed these meats without any apparent health problems. But without conclusive evidence either way, it's difficult to assess the safety of this wood for barbecuing. The flavor, however, is sensational.

Pecan. Pecan seems to be the principle wood from the nut-bearing trees that has gained popularity. Pecan, along with the other woods mentioned, are current favorites of Kansas City barbecuers. Pecan-smoked foods have a particular delicate flavor. In addition, pecan doesn't seem to produce the sooty residues that other woods do.

CHARCOAL: THAT OLD BLACK MAGIC

Perhaps as early as 300,000 B.C. somebody discovered that charred wood burned better than uncharred wood, and prehistoric man may have looked for ways to make more of it. Eventually someone covered fire with earth to prevent complete combustion and lo, the art of making charcoal was born. Today, however, the majority of those who do outdoor cooking far prefer the use of charcoal briquets to the lump charcoal used by our prehistoric ancestors.

Yet briquets were rarely used before World War II except for commercial uses. It took Henry Ford to turn the charcoal briquet into a household necessity. In the early '20s, Ford couldn't buy wood alcohol except at very high prices. The Ford plant badly needed alcohol to use in the manufacturing of automobiles, so Ford brought in a chemist who proceeded to come up with a grand idea for wood distillation.

A modern plant was set up and 80,000 acres of woodland were purchased for the venture. The Ford Chemical Plant was equipped with everything to chip, char, and dry wood. Soon alcohol by the carloads was being generated from wood distillation. There was, unfortunately, the troublesome by-product of charcoal to deal with. Henry came up with yet another idea: why not make one uniform product of charcoal and sell it all over the country?

Automatic briquetting machinery was installed and the new Ford Charcoal Briquets soon were coming off the presses every day. Among the first to realize the potential and long-burning qualities were foundries, then hotels and restaurants who realized that briquets were an excellent medium for broiling. The first briquets were sold at Ford auto dealers! Later, Ford's associate Charles Kingsford bought out the charcoal business.

Today the availability of charcoal briquets has made outdoor cooking a national pastime, and Missouri is the nation's largest producer of hardwood charcoal and charcoal briquets. As consumers have discovered, the quality of charcoal briquets can vary greatly. Most are a blend of hardwood charcoal with anthracite or sawdust, a lighting ingredient, and starch binders. The greater the percentage of hardwood charcoal, the better the charcoal briquet.

According to John Uhlmann, whose Kansas City–based company created Patio Chef Charcoal Briquets, there are several things to consider when purchasing briquets: "The charcoal needs to light in a reasonable period of time and should be 80 percent ashed over and ready to cook in at least 30 minutes," he says. "It should also reach a minimum of 425 degrees within 30 minutes and be at 350 degrees or hotter for at least one hour."

Uhlmann points out that the flavor you taste is actually caused by the wood charcoal in the briquets. These volatiles or flavor agents are in the wood itself, which is what is captured as the wood is converted into charcoal. "It is important to remember to let the coals get at least 80 percent ashed over to avoid the taste of lighter fuel," he says. "Too often people start cooking before the coal is properly ashed."

RUBS, MARINADES, AND SAUCES

Liquid smoke. There are many varieties of liquid smoke, including hickory- and mesquite-flavored products. While not particularly loved by the serious barbecuer, nevertheless they come in handy when you can't cook outdoors. Made by burning wood, the liquid smoke is processed and filtered through water and harmful ingredients are extracted from it. Approved by the FDA, liquid smoke works well for barbecued beans, indoor ribs, and brisket, but it can't substitute for a table sauce, and it shouldn't be used "raw" since it has a bitter taste.

Liquid smoke can be combined with water, in a ratio of two parts water to one part liquid smoke, and the meat marinated in this solution for 30 to 60 minutes. Remove and cook the food in the usual manner. You'll notice that there is a reasonable facsimile of smoke flavor, although it really doesn't come close to an honest-to-goodness hunk of outdoor barbecued beef.

To marinate meat in a liquid solution, always use noncorrosive glass, stainless steel, or ceramic or plastic containers, including heavy-duty, resealable plastic bags. Never use aluminum or other metals. Place in the refrigerator and turn occasionally.

Dry rubs. The three basic ingredients often used for dry rubs include salt, paprika, and black pepper, followed by varying amounts of sugar, chili powder, garlic powder, and other spices such as red pepper (if you can stand the heat). Dry rubs describe a mixture of barbecue spices that are rubbed on meats before cooking. Other ingredients such as cumin or powdered mustard add to the list of endless possibilities. Dried herbs can produce sublime results when added to rubs; try rosemary or sweet basil for a lamb rub, oregano for an Italian-style rub, and sage for a beef rub.

Dry rubs are also excellent for indoor barbecuing. Some of them also include powdered smoke, making it possible to get outdoor wood flavor, a passable imitation of the real thing.

Many barbecuers caution against the use of salt in rubs. Salt, they say, can toughen meat and dry it out. It all boils down to the method of cooking: If you cook at a higher heat, over a long period of time, then a great deal of liquid can be extracted from any food. Slow cooking at a low temperature forces less juice out of the meat that is sealed with an external dry rub. The searing process, too, tends to seal any food that is cooked fast on a grill, such as steaks or hamburgers, preventing juice loss.

Often cooks will utilize a thin layer of prepared mustard before applying a dry rub. The mustard contains vinegar, which is a natural tenderizer. A mustard that is both hot and sweet works well with a rub that includes brown sugar and paprika. The dry rub also may contain garlic, which further seasons the meat.

While there are some chefs who swear by the paprika/brown sugar and spices combination, there are those who cook ribs, chicken, and pork using only pepper or nothing at all. They insist the taste comes from the ultimate control of the temperature and smoking process.

Marinades. According to Webster's, one definition of barbecue is "to cook in a highly seasoned vinegar sauce." Not that everyone would agree. Many purists would never barbecue with mixtures of beer or soy sauce, nor do they use stovetop blends of butter and wine. These mixtures aren't like the blends of peppers and spices used for barbecuing. And, while Asian-inspired sauces may produce an excellent taste, don't confuse them with traditional American barbecue.

Many people don't realize there is a definite difference between marinades and red tomato-based table sauces. It's like comparing apples and applesauce. Each is wonderful in its own way, but distinctly different.

In states where barbecue is a way of life, marinades and table sauces often complement each other. Traditionally marinades are acidic or vinegar-based, spicy mixtures that tenderize the meat and cook through it instead of burning onto it. Many people baste the meat the last 20 minutes with a red sauce to give it a crusty glaze. The red sauce is usually offered at the table. (It should be noted that, in some circles, putting a red sauce on a hickory-smoked marinated chicken may be viewed as akin to putting mayonnaise on Peking duck.)

Marinades were traditionally used in such states as the Carolinas, Arkansas, Tennessee, Mississippi, and Kentucky, and in other areas of the South. Their appeal has become universal, with whole books being written on the subject. Many people make their own marinades using a blend of oil, vinegar, and spices. Some add vinegar to packets of dry marinades, and others simply buy it ready-made.

The beauty of a marinade is that it can make tougher cuts of meat, such as flank or round steak and brisket, taste like a rich man's bounty. It also works well for pork, chicken, and fish, wild game, and beef tenderloin. The secret is to marinate tougher cuts well before putting them on the grill, then basting throughout the cooking time.

Following are some tips for cooking with dry rubs and marinades:

Brisket: marinate overnight, then cook on a slow grill (225 degrees) and baste every 60 minutes with marinade until done (between 8 and 15 hours, depending on weight).

Chicken: marinate for 2 hours, then cook on a medium fire (250 to 300 degrees), basting the pieces with marinade every time you turn them, until done. (Be sure to cook off the last of the marinade after the last dipping.)

Game: marinate for 2 hours to overnight, depending on the cut of meat, then cook on a slow grill (225 degrees) and baste every 30 minutes with marinade until done.

Lamb: marinate for 2 hours (you can use the leg, chops or shank). Baste every 30 minutes at 200 to 225 degrees until done. Try using a sprig of rosemary as your "basting brush."

Pork ribs: marinate for at least 2 hours and baste frequently (every 30 minutes) on a low fire (220 to 225 degrees) for around 4 to 5 hours.

Seafood and fish: do not marinate more than 30 minutes. A good rule of thumb for grilling is 10 minutes per inch of thickness over a medium-hot fire.

BARBECUE SAUCES (RED TABLE SAUCES)

The flavor and style of Kansas City's spicy barbecue sauces are virtually unlimited. A sampling of sauces available in supermarkets, restaurants, and gift shops around the city reads like a local and national who's who of the barbecue business. There are probably more varieties of barbecue sauce available in Kansas City than any other city in the United States. One local supermarket carries over 60 varieties and sizes of barbecue sauces. Add to this the local barbecue restaurants that sell their sauce on-site, and you've got a virtual Valhalla for lovers of the stuff.

Very few places in the Midwest use the pure Eastern, Carolinas-style sauce, consisting primarily of peppers in a bottle with vinegar, although some of these are available locally. The majority of successful red sauces are usually variations on the theme of tomato base (in the form of ketchup or tomato puree), sweeteners such as brown sugar or molasses, hot spices, and the occasional use of liquid smoke.

★ MEAT BASICS: BRISKET AND RIBS ★

Beef brisket and pork ribs are the two most common cuts for barbecuing. Before you put either on the grill, there are some useful things to know and remember.

BRISKET

The whole brisket is a belly muscle of beef, which is tough enough to need tenderizing before you cook it. There are two ways to tenderize this unusually tough piece of meat: You can use a dry rub or marinade to help break down the fibers, and you can cook the meat slowly.

A whole brisket weighs between 5 and 12 pounds untrimmed. It has a thick end or "point" and a thin or "flat" end. The brisket is covered with fat on one side and has another large layer of fat that extends inside the point end. The fat acts as a natural baste and adds an excellent taste to the meat as it cooks. Once the meat is done, the fat may be trimmed and discarded.

RIBS

The very choicest ribs for barbecuing are determined by two factors: location of the ribs, and weight and size of the ribs. If you're confused about barbecued pork ribs and the various names used to identify them, and you want to know how spareribs differ from loin ribs, country back ribs, and baby back ribs, just refer to the drawings on p. xxxii.

The whole slab of spareribs can be cut in half. Then you have the smaller (or short end) ribs on one half, and the large (or long end) ribs on the other. Untrimmed spareribs are great, but they have more bone, gristle, and fat. (That's why they are the cheapest rib cut.) When the chine bone and brisket are trimmed off the sparerib, you have the St. Louis, or "Kelso," cut.

Loin pork ribs look somewhat like the trimmed St. Louis cut, but they are different. Loin ribs are generally the preferred cut and require less trimming because they are meatier. Be sure to remove the membrane from the underside of the ribs before applying rubs and marinades and cooking.

The weight of the entire slab determines the choicest meatiest ribs, regardless of whether they are loin or spareribs. Since small weight slabs of ribs are usually meatier, they are considered the best and most expensive.

When the whole, untrimmed slabs of either loin or sparerib are weighed, they are grouped and named according to four major weights: whole slabs weighing under two pounds being called "two and under," followed by "three and under," "three to five," and "five pounds and over."

Therefore, loin pork ribs (meatiest cut), two pounds and under (meatiest

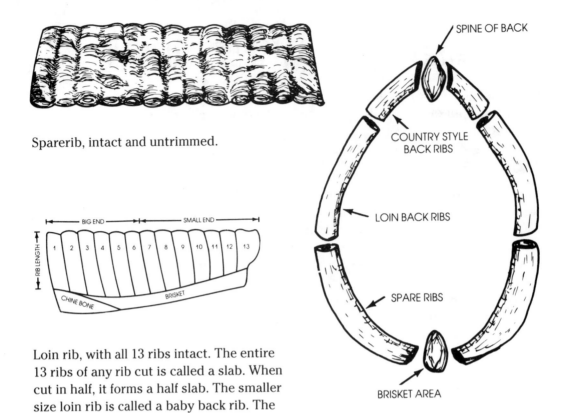

Sparerib, intact and untrimmed.

Loin rib, with all 13 ribs intact. The entire 13 ribs of any rib cut is called a slab. When cut in half, it forms a half slab. The smaller size loin rib is called a baby back rib. The "Danish rib" is a variety of baby back rib.

The three main anatomical rib cuts—country back, loin, and sparerib.

weight), are the choicest (baby back ribs). The country-style back ribs are also meaty, but have more bone per pound. St. Louis–cut and spareribs are next in line. Still, if you can afford it, the small loin (baby back) ribs are tops for the money.

BARBECUED RIBS KANSAS CITY–STYLE

Now that we've reviewed the basics, the following step-by step methods for preparing barbecued ribs should tie it all together.

To fix ribs using the *outdoor* method:

1. Place a chimney fire-starter in your barbecue unit.

2. Place crushed newspaper in the bottom section and put 12 to 15 charcoal briquets in the top part of the chimney. (Use 100 percent hardwood charcoal for the best results). Light the newspapers in the lower section.

3. Take three whole slabs of loin back pork ribs, preferably two pounds and

under. Season with a dry rub (or coat ribs on all sides lightly with prepared mustard), then sprinkle generously with paprika and dark brown sugar, plus some cracked black pepper if you like.

4. Add two premoistened hickory chunks when the coals are red.

5. Do not spread the charcoal out as for grilling. Place ribs fat-side up in the smoker, away from the fire, and close the lid, leaving the damper barely open. Do not open the lid except to add more briquets and wood chunks. You won't need a heavy smoke if you're planning to barbecue for several hours. Some smoke should be seeping from the edges of the smoker, or from the barely opened damper, at all times.

6. Don't allow the fire to flare. Occasionally when you open the lid to add briquets, it may flame up. This usually subsides when the lid is closed tightly, but a spray of water away from the food will put out the flame. Remember that such a fire is much too hot for barbecuing.

7. Smoke-cook at 225 degrees for 4 to 6 hours. Ribs can be stacked and rotated to maintain juices for self-basting. They do not need turning unless the fire has gotten too hot and has overbrowned a side.

8. Turn the ribs during the last 20 minutes (fat-side down), baste generously with barbecue sauce, and let smoke. Use about a half cup of sauce per slab.

9. Let the ribs cool down enough to handle, and then serve them with additional barbecue sauce on the side.

To fix ribs using the *indoor* method:

1. Parboil the ribs (optional) or cook them as they are.

2. Coat the ribs with liquid hickory smoke (2 tablespoons in 4 tablespoons of water per slab). Cover the ribs with the same mustard or dry rub mentioned in the outdoor method.

3. Preheat the oven to 400 degrees. Place the ribs fat-side up on a rack in a pan and cook for 15 minutes. Reduce the heat to 250 degrees and cook for another 2 hours.

4. Baste with your favorite barbecue sauce and cook for an additional 30 minutes.

★ THE 10 COMMANDMENTS OF GOOD BARBECUE ★

Now it's time to get out and barbecue, Kansas City–style. Here are the highlights to remember before you put dinner on the grill:

1. SMOKE IT SLOW AND KEEP THE FIRE LOW

Legitimate, native American barbecue, including Kansas City–style barbecue, requires patience and a slow hand. Use low heat (175 to 225 degrees), and, ideally, smoke from live wood or charcoal fires. Use open-pit methods for lightly smoked meat or closed-pit methods for heavily smoked meat. This way, the meat is both cooked and smoked until well done.

It is impossible to prepare a genuine Kansas City barbecued brisket in less than 8 hours—that's the bare minimum (many a prize-winning brisket will barbecue for 10 to 20 hours).

2. USE HIGH HEAT ONLY WHEN GRILLING OR SEARING

Place meat directly over a hot fire only to grill it or to sear it. Cover the grill and leave the air vents open to allow for oxygen flow to the fire. This will increase the heat.

3. DON'T TRIM THE FAT OFF BRISKET AND RIBS BEFORE SMOKING

Traditionally it's essential that you leave the fat on the meat during barbecuing to continually moisten and baste it. Cook the meat fat-side up and keep it as far from the fire as possible in order to get a 200- to 225-degree temperature at meat level. Over the hours in the heat, much of the fat drips away. When the food is done, trim off or cut out the remaining fat before slicing the meat or serving the ribs.

When a brisket has cooled, raise the upper layer of the cooked meat and slice out the excess fat, then slice the remaining meat. There is enough crispness left on the surface of the brisket so you'll get both the juicy, well-smoked, well-done interior as well as the crisp exterior. The perfect barbecued ribs in Kansas City are described as having a touch of char on the end and a darkened, almost crisp coating on part of the outside. The interior of the rib remains moist if not overly trimmed, even with a crusty outside.

4. REMEMBER THAT TRADITIONALLY BARBECUED MEATS ARE WELL DONE

Any pinkness you see in fully cooked barbecued meats results from the slow smoking. Some contemporary barbecuers will smoke-cook whole beef tenderloin for just an hour to leave the interior medium-rare, but this might be called "nouvelle barbecue."

5. DON'T CONFUSE GRILLING WITH BARBECUING

Barbecuing—that is, slow smoke-cooking—is always done with the charcoal or hardwood fire positioned at some distance from the meat. This is difficult to achieve with the round barbecue cookers in which the fire in the center sits directly under the food. When using this type of cooker for barbecue, bank your fire to one side and place your meat on the opposite side. It's also essential that the coals be lowered as far as possible from the grill or the grill elevated well above the goals.

Many barbecue aficionados recommend using a water smoker, or you can just place an aluminum pan of water in the center of a round unit, build the charcoal fire around the edges, and then position the meat above the water pan. The only drawback to the water smoker method, according to several barbecue contest winners, is that too much heat under the water pan tends to steam the meat and can eliminate the crusty exterior.

6. CONSIDER THE WIND AND THE OUTDOOR TEMPERATURE

Barbecuing a brisket in summer with the sun bearing down on your setup will cook foods far more rapidly. This also tends to dry them out, since the unit is heated by both the sun and the charcoal. Barbecuing outdoors in winter (which many Kansas Citians do regularly) eliminates one of these heat sources, so additional charcoal or a longer cooking time has to make up the difference.

Also take the wind into consideration. A good barbecue unit is reasonably well sealed, relying on a vent to provide more or less air to heighten the fire. There is also some inlet of air to keep the fire from going out. However, on a gusty day, with the wind forcing itself into various crevices and niches that ordinarily don't produce much exchange of air, your charcoal will burn hotter and thus your meat will cook more rapidly.

A cold wind can really create a dilemma. The cold lowers the heat, and the wind increases the flame and heat. By learning to balance (and compensate for) these elements, you'll be able to produce the kind of barbecue you want every time.

7. LEARN WHEN TO USE SAUCES

Marinate in vinegar-based liquid or dry rub, yes. But marinate in a red table sauce? Definitely not. This is particularly true for tomato-based and heavily sweetened barbecue sauces. Both tomato and sugar tend to burn and turn black at reasonably low temperatures, so having barbecue sauce on the meat at the beginning of the cooking process is an error in our estimation.

Besides the issue of marinating, although most people would not consider cooking asparagus in Hollandaise sauce, many see nothing wrong with basting barbecued meats continuously with tomatoey sauces. To barbecue pros, this is sacrilege! There is one exception to this commandment that many Kansas Citians make, though: They baste during the last 20 minutes or so with their favorite barbecue sauce, which seals the meat and produces an excellent aroma and taste. A few prefer to brush on a tomato-based sauce mixed with honey, and some of these bastes can heighten flavor and moisture. But only try this if the fire is low enough and if you prefer a bit of charring on the outside of your meat. (And check the meat regularly so it doesn't burn.)

Barbecue sauces are generally served at the table, so people can add them if they prefer.

8. MAKE THE BEST USE OF WOOD

Select your woods based on availability, cost, and flavor. Mesquite produces the hottest fire. Hickory is most readily available and produces a heavy smoke flavor. Fruitwood has a mellow taste. Never use pine or other resinous soft woods. Wood chips and sawdust are fine for grilling; chunks are best for barbecuing.

When grilling, add water-soaked chips directly to the coals. The longer the wood soaks before used in cooking, the better the smoke. Small chips should sit in water at least 30 minutes; big chunks of wood at least 10 to 12 hours.

9. USE CHARCOAL BRIQUETS PROPERLY

A small charcoal fire for covered smoke-cooking provides an excellent heat source as well as a means of producing smoke from the wood. Heat doesn't escape as it does with open barbecuing, and a little fuel goes a long way.

You can start with between 12 and 25 briquets in your kettle, which should last from 1 to 2 hours. Add more briquets as needed. (Always allow your charcoal to ash down before starting to cook.) Serious barbecuers use cookers that have the advantage of fireboxes that provide for easy loading of additional charcoal and wood.

10. BRING MEAT TO ROOM TEMPERATURE BEFORE COOKING

Starting with your meat at room temperature allows for more dependable cooking time, which in turn produces much better barbecue. The important exceptions to this rule, however, are fish, seafood, and poultry, which for health reasons should be kept chilled until you're ready to put them on the grill.

RECIPES

★ ★ ★ ★

**A sampling from Kansas City's pitmasters
and backyard barons of barbecue**

BEEF

★ ★ ★ ★

The best steaks for grilling contain the greatest degree of marbling. Lower priced, less tender cuts are ideal for marinating and smoking.

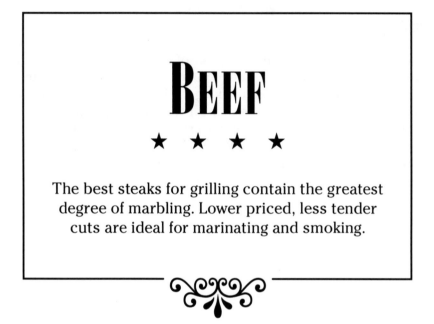

BLUE RIBBON BEEF BRISKET

DAVE HALSEY

1 (5-pound) brisket, cut in half
Teriyaki sauce (enough to cover meat)
Morton's Nature's Seasons to taste
1 (12-ounce) can beer, room temperature
K.C. Masterpiece barbecue sauce (original)

Marinate brisket halves overnight in a mixture of teriyaki sauce and Morton's seasoning.

Arrange coals along sides of grill and let heat for 45 minutes. Stack brisket halves one on top of the other in the center of the grill and leave in this position for 10 minutes with the lid closed, cooking at 300 degrees. Rotate meat, putting top half on the bottom and cooking for 10 minutes more. Repeat this process for both sides of each piece of meat (this sealing process takes a total of 40 minutes). Continue to rotate meat every 20 to 30 minutes at 225 degrees for 6 to 8 hours, basting with beer to keep moist on the outside. Baste with barbecue sauce during the final 30 minutes, turning meat every 5 minutes to avoid burning.

Serves 8

INDOOR BARBECUED MARINATED BEEF BRISKET

RICH DAVIS

Plan ahead for this one—you don't eat it 'til the third day!

1 (5- to 8-pound) brisket
1/4 cup liquid smoke
1/4 cup Worcestershire sauce
1/3 cup Italian salad dressing
1/4 cup liquid B-V (or other liquid beef concentrate)
1 tablespoon finely minced garlic
1 (18-ounce) bottle K.C. Masterpiece barbecue sauce (original) plus
  additional for serving

Place brisket on a large sheet of foil in a large baking dish. Mix liquid smoke, Worcestershire, salad dressing, B-V, and garlic with 1 cup of barbecue sauce and pour over brisket. Let sit for 15 minutes, then seal foil around meat completely. Place in the refrigerator to marinate overnight.

Bring meat to room temperature (still covered in dish). Preheat oven to 350 degrees. Without uncovering meat, bake for 4 hours. Cool, then return to refrigerator overnight.

Remove meat from foil and discard fat. Slice brisket across the grain and cover with remaining barbecue sauce. Reheat at 350 degrees for 30 minutes. Serve with additional sauce.

Serves 8

BARBECUED WHOLE TENDERLOIN
RICH DAVIS

This recipe won first prize at the Colorado Beef Growers' contest using beef tenderloin, and first prize at the American Royal Barbecue Contest in 1980 using whole pork tenderloin.

5 to 7 pounds whole trimmed beef tenderloin (or 3 large pork tenderloins), room temperature

MARINADE
1 cup soy sauce
1/3 cup sesame oil
3 large cloves garlic, minced
1 tablespoon ground ginger

SAUCE
1 (18-ounce) bottle K.C. Masterpiece barbecue sauce (any label)
1/3 cup soy sauce
1/4 cup sesame oil
1 large clove garlic, finely minced

Combine marinade ingredients and marinate tenderloins overnight in the refrigerator.

Place tenderloins on a prepared charcoal grill (with moistened hickory chips added to smoke) over low fire, turning every 15 minutes and basting with reserved marinade. Barbecue with lid closed until beef is done to preferred rareness (or approximately 1-1/2 hours for pork; use a meat thermometer).

(*Note:* For indoor barbecuing, rub tenderloins generously with liquid hickory or mesquite smoke, marinate overnight in above mixture, then cook in a 300-degree preheated oven, following basting directions above to desired doneness.)

Combine sauce ingredients, stir well, and heat gently. Serve warm with meat.

Serves 8

SAVORY BEEF TENDERLOIN
BETTY GOSS

5 to 7 pounds whole trimmed beef tenderloin
1/2 cup (1 stick) butter, melted
1 (18-ounce) bottle barbecue sauce
2 teaspoons garlic salt

Marinate tenderloin overnight (refrigerated) in combined butter, barbecue sauce, and garlic salt.

Remove tenderloin, reserving the marinade. Grill meat over prepared coals for 15 minutes on each side over a hot fire and hickory chips.

Remove tenderloin and place on foil wrap in a baking pan. Pour remaining marinade over meat and seal foil tightly. Bake for 1 hour at 300 degrees (less time for rarer meat). Unwrap, slice, and serve.

Serves 6–8

ITALIAN-STYLE STRIP STEAKS

4 Kansas City strip steaks
4 tablespoons olive oil

SPICE RUB
1 tablespoon garlic salt
1 tablespoon paprika
2 teaspoons dried basil
2 teaspoons dried oregano
1/2 tablespoon ground black pepper
1 teaspoon ground red pepper

Combine spice rub ingredients and set aside. Lightly coat each steak with 1 tablespoon of oil, then rub on spice mix until well coated. Let meat stand at room temperature for 1 hour, then grill over hot coals for 4 to 6 minutes on each side.

Serves 4

SIRLOIN STEAK BOURBON-CUE

BOB BURROWS

This is a token "cheater" for people who hate to take the time to barbecue. The steak, coated with alcohol and brown sugar, will flame on the grill, so use a long-handled fork for turning and wear gloves. The barbecue sauce will be sucked right into the bourbon-laced meat, and you get a sirloin that is burned black on the outside and very rare on the inside. Serve with a tart salad and a baked potato.

1 (2-pound) sirloin steak, 1-1/2 inches thick
1 cup Kentucky bourbon
1/2 cup liquid brown sugar
1/4 cup (1/2 stick) butter
Barbecue sauce

In a glass dish large enough to hold the steak, combine bourbon and liquid brown sugar. Marinate meat in mixture for 2 hours in the refrigerator. (Do not turn meat during this time.)

Remove from refrigerator, turn steak over, and marinate on the other side for an additional 2 hours at room temperature.

Drain steak and reserve marinade. Prepare a very hot grill. Melt butter and combine with reserved marinade and enough barbecue sauce to make a mixture of loose consistency. Dip both sides of steak in mixture and grill for 6 to 8 minutes on each side (until crusty).

Serves 2

GARLIC MARINATED SIRLOIN STEAK

2 (3-pound) sirloin steaks, 1-1/4 to 2 inches thick
1/3 cup Worcestershire sauce
2 teaspoons granulated garlic
2 teaspoons lemon pepper

Coat steaks with Worcestershire sauce and rub on dry ingredients. Marinate meat in the refrigerator for 2 hours.

Bring steaks to room temperature and sear for 2 minutes on each side over hot coals. Reduce heat to medium by spreading coals out and cook to taste (rare, 4 minutes each side; medium, 6 minutes each side; well done, 8 minutes each side).

Serves 8–10

MARINATED SMOKED FLANK STEAK

KAREN PUTMAN

1 (3- to 5-pound) flank steak

MARINADE
1 quart Coca-Cola
2 cups vegetable oil
2 cups white vinegar
6 cloves garlic, minced
Salt and pepper to taste

Combine marinade ingredients and marinate meat in the refrigerator overnight.

Remove steak (reserving marinade) and smoke at 200 degrees for 6 to 8 hours, basting every 20 to 30 minutes with reserved marinade.

Serves 6–8

KANSAS CITY FAJITAS WITH SALSA ALICIA

CHARLES BARSOTTI

1 (3-pound) skirt steak or flank steak
1 (16-ounce) bottle Italian dressing
Flour tortillas

Marinate meat in Italian dressing for about 4 hours in the refrigerator.

Drain steak and grill over hot coals and mesquite chips for 20 minutes, or until meat reaches preferred doneness. Slice steak into small strips, smother with Salsa Alicia, wrap in warm flour tortillas, and serve.

Serves 6

SALSA ALICIA

3 strips bacon, cut into small pieces
1/2 cup chopped onion
1/2 cup chopped green bell pepper
1 (16-ounce) can whole tomatoes, diced (reserve liquid)
1 teaspoon salt
2 or 3 chopped jalapeño peppers

Fry bacon, then add onion and green peppers and sauté. Add tomatoes with liquid, salt, and jalapeño peppers. Simmer on low heat for 20 minutes, then set aside until ready to serve.

Makes about 2 cups

BARBECUED RIB ROAST

PAUL KIRK

1 (7-pound) boneless rib roast
Lemon pepper

MARINADE
1/2 cup water
1-1/2 cups Burgundy
1/2 cup red wine vinegar
1 medium onion, sliced thinly
4 stalks celery, diced
2 cloves garlic, crushed
2 bay leaves, crushed

Combine marinade ingredients and simmer for 20 minutes. Remove from heat. Rub roast generously with lemon pepper, then place meat and marinade mixture in a large resealable plastic bag. Marinate in the refrigerator for 4 hours.

Prepare fire on one side of the grill. Remove roast from bag and place at opposite end of grill from the fire. Cover and cook at 150 degrees for 2-1/2 hours or 25 minutes per pound. Add moistened hickory chunks to the fire periodically.

Serves 14–20

BARBECUED STUFFED CABBAGE ROLLS

RICH DAVIS

1-1/2 pounds lean ground beef
1-1/2 pounds ground turkey
1/2 cup cooked rice
1-1/2 teaspoons salt
1 teaspoon cracked black pepper
1 tablespoon minced garlic
2 tablespoons Worcestershire sauce
1/2 cup chopped green bell pepper
1 (12-ounce) can Ro-Tel chopped tomatoes and chilies, drained
3 cups chopped onion
2 eggs, lightly beaten
1/2 cup crushed saltine crackers
2 or 3 heads cabbage (enough to yield 36 large leaves)
3-1/2 cups K.C. Masterpiece barbecue sauce (original)

Mix together by hand ground beef, ground turkey, rice, salt, pepper, garlic, Worcestershire sauce, green peppers, tomatoes and chilies, 1 cup of onion, eggs, and crackers. Set aside.

Cut out and discard hard centers of cabbages. Place heads in a large pot and cover with boiling water. Simmer over low heat until leaves can be easily removed, about 7 or 8 minutes.

Preheat oven to 350 degrees. Roll meat mixture into 36 sausage-like shapes, about 3 inches long and 1 inch thick. Place each meat roll on a cabbage leaf and fold leaf over stuffing, tucking in ends to seal. Thoroughly grease two 9-by-13-inch baking dishes. Spread remaining onion over bottoms of each dish, then top with rows of cabbage rolls, seam-side down. Pour 3 cups of barbecue sauce evenly over rolls and cover pan tightly with foil. Bake for 1 hour. Remove foil and baste rolls with pan juices. Uncover and bake for an additional 15 minutes. Serve with remaining barbecue sauce spooned over rolls.

Serves 12–15

PORK

★　★　★　★

The loin is the most prized cut of pork,
but flavorful and economical options include
shoulder, roasts, and ham, all perfect for
slow-smoked barbecuing.

COUNTRY-STYLE RIBS

LINDSAY SHANNON

Serve these ribs with a bowl of sauce, your favorite bread, fresh vegetables, and Avery Island Potato Pancakes (p. 76).

2 slabs country-style pork ribs
Black pepper to taste
Barbecue sauce

Separate ribs if necessary and put into a large pot of boiling water for 5 minutes (this breaks down the tough parts of the meat and you won't lose flavor). Sprinkle ribs with black pepper and let sit at room temperature for 30 minutes. Soak hickory chips in water during this time.

Add hickory chips to hot coals. Place ribs in smoker at opposite end away from fire. Keep lid down and slow cook for 2-1/2 to 3 hours at 200 to 225 degrees. After smoking, put ribs directly over low fire for a few minutes on each side. Apply a coat of barbecue sauce just before taking off the grill.

Serves 4–6

BLUE RIBBON BARBECUED COUNTRY BACK RIBS

DAVE HALSEY

2 slabs country back pork ribs
Teriyaki sauce (enough to cover ribs)
Morton's Nature's Seasons to taste
1 (12-ounce) can beer, room temperature
K.C. Masterpiece barbecue sauce (original)

Do not trim fat from ribs or parboil. Marinate overnight in the refrigerator in a mixture of teriyaki sauce and Morton's seasoning.

Prepare coals around sides of grill and let ash down, about 45 minutes. Stack ribs, one on top of the other, in the center of the grill. Leave in this position for 10 minutes, with the lid closed, at 300 degrees. Rotate the stack, putting top slab on the bottom, and cook for 10 minutes more. Repeat the process on the other side of each slab of ribs. (This takes 40 minutes in all.) Allow heat to lower to 225 degrees and continue rotating slabs, occasionally basting with beer to keep ribs moist on the outside. Turn every 20 to 30 minutes for about 2 hours. Baste with barbecue sauce for another hour, continuing to rotate ribs and letting fire die out naturally.

Serves 4–6

HICKORY-SMOKED BARBECUED RIBS

RICH DAVIS

If there's any left, these are delicious cold the next day.

2 slabs loin baby back pork ribs
Prepared yellow mustard
Ground black pepper
Hungarian paprika
Dark brown sugar
Salt
K.C. Masterpiece barbecue sauce (original)

Lightly rub ribs all over with mustard. Sprinkle lightly with pepper on both sides, then sprinkle generously with paprika on both sides. Crumble dark brown sugar onto both sides of ribs and press into meat. Place ribs on rack, fat-side up, away from charcoal fire containing water-soaked hickory chunks. Smoke for 4 to 5 hours at 200 to 225 degrees. Check fire occasionally to prevent ribs from turning black. No need to turn ribs during cooking.

During last 30 minutes, salt ribs and coat tops generously with barbecue sauce. Serve when cool enough to handle.

Serves 6

BARBECUED SPARERIBS

STEVE STEPHENSON

Serve these succulent ribs with Stephenson's Barbecue Sauce on the side (recipe on p. 62).

5 to 6 slabs pork spareribs
1 cup salt
1 cup barbecue seasoning
1 cup monosodium glutamate or Accent (optional)
1 cup paprika

Prepare grill and let coals turn almost white. Starting at one end, cut each rib almost to the top. On a big plate, mix seasonings together. Lay ribs on one side of the plate. Cover with mixture, and press as much into meat as possible. Flip ribs, cover with seasoning mixture, and press mixture into meat as before. Lay ribs in a smoker or on the grill. Cook for 15 minutes, then turn over and cook for 15 minutes on the other side. Continue to flip every 15 minutes. Cook until ribs pull apart easily, about 2-1/2 hours at 225 degrees.

Serves 10–14

INDOOR BABY BACK RIBS

KITTY BERKOWITZ

Delicious, with an outdoor smoky flavor!

4 pounds baby back pork ribs
1/4 cup liquid smoke
1/4 cup tomato sauce
3/4 cup Old Southern Hickory Smoke barbecue sauce
1 teaspoon salt

Place ribs in a baking pan. Combine remaining ingredients, pour over both sides of ribs, and let stand for 1 hour at room temperature.

Preheat oven to 500 degrees. Place uncovered ribs in hot oven for 10 minutes. Reduce temperature to 250 degrees, cover, and bake for 2 hours, basting occasionally. Cool slightly and serve.

Serves 4

INDOOR BARBECUED RIBS

TOM LEATHERS

1 (3-pound) slab pork spareribs
Liquid smoke
Barbecue sauce

With a sharp knife, remove membrane from underside of ribs. Remove all fat. Spread liquid smoke on both sides of ribs, then place in a pan, cover with foil, and bake for 1-1/2 to 2 hours at 275 degrees. Pour off most of the liquid in the pan. Spread barbecue sauce on both sides of ribs. Cover again and continue cooking for about 2 hours more, until ribs are extremely tender. Remove foil for last 15 minutes of cooking time.

Serves 2–3

INDOOR/OUTDOOR RIBS

ART SIEMERING

4 pounds pork ribs or beef short ribs
1/2 cup strong-flavored beer, room temperature
4 tablespoons light molasses
2 teaspoons Maggi gravy seasoning or similar product (such as Kitchen Bouquet)
1 teaspoon liquid smoke
1 teaspoon sesame oil
8 slices white bread
Kansas City–style barbecue sauce

Place ribs in a large roasting pan. Pour beer around ribs and cover pan tightly with lid or heavy-duty foil. Bake at 400 degrees for 1 hour. Combine molasses, gravy seasoning, liquid smoke, and sesame oil, and set aside. Remove ribs from oven, then remove from pan and pat dry with paper towels.

To finish ribs in the broiler, place on a rack, meaty-side up, and brush generously with browning sauce. Place rack 4 to 6 inches from heat and broil for 4 to 5 minutes, or until browned to taste. Turn ribs, brush with more sauce, and broil.

To finish on a barbecue grill, brush with browning sauce and grill over hot coals for 6 minutes, or until ribs are well charred.

To serve, arrange each portion over 2 slices of bread and paint generously with barbecue sauce.

Serves 4

CHAMPIONSHIP BARBECUED SPARERIBS
GUY SIMPSON AND MARVIN DAVIS

1 slab pork spareribs
Liquid smoke
Garlic salt
Celery salt
Pepper
1 (12-ounce) can beer, room temperature
Barbecue sauce

Pull membrane from top of ribs and fatty meat portion. Lightly sprinkle liquid smoke on both sides of ribs and rub in by hand, then lightly sprinkle spices over both sides. Place on smoker or pit and cook over indirect heat for about 2-1/2 hours, or until bone is exposed about 1/2 inch on the end. Turn ribs every 45 minutes and keep moist by dabbing occasionally with beer. Baste with barbecue sauce during last 30 minutes.

Serves 2

BLUE RIBBON BARBECUED PORK SHOULDER

DAVE HALSEY

1 (3- to 5-pound) pork shoulder, bone in
Teriyaki sauce (enough to cover meat)
Morton's Nature's Seasons to taste
1 (12-ounce) can beer, room temperature
K.C. Masterpiece barbecue sauce (original)

Marinate meat in a mixture of teriyaki sauce and Morton's seasoning overnight in the refrigerator.

Arrange coals around edges of the grill and ash down for 45 minutes. Seal roast by turning every 10 minutes at 300 degrees (lid closed) until all exposed sides are seared. Let fire cool down to 225 degrees and continue turning meat every 20 to 30 minutes, basting occasionally with beer, for about 2-1/2 hours. Cook for 30 minutes more, basting with barbecue sauce and turning every 5 minutes so meat doesn't burn.

Serves 6–12

PRIZE-WINNING HONEY-SMOKED PORK LOIN
DICK MAIS

Dick recommends smoking this meat over a combination of hickory and mesquite. He also believes that the finest way to enjoy the pork loin is with a Southern-style mustard-based sauce or one that contains such important flavorings as apple cider vinegar, onions, soy sauce, sugar, and blended peppers.

1-1/2 cups honey
1 (3- to 6-pound) Canadian pork loin
1/2 cup prepared mustard
Dry barbecue spice rub
Barbecue sauce (optional)

Heat honey until it becomes the consistency of water (don't boil). Using a large bore needle and syringe, inject pork loin with honey in at least 4 different sites. Cover loin with mustard and dry rub. Wrap meat in foil and let it marinate in the refrigerator for at least 6 hours.

Remove loin and allow to reach room temperature. Smoke meat at 175 degrees for 12 hours (if your unit runs hotter than this, keep heat as low as possible and smoke for 6 to 8 hours). If desired, glaze loin with barbecue sauce during last half hour of cooking time.

Serves 6–12

HICKORY-GRILLED PORK BURGER
MARTY'S BAR-B-Q

1 pound lean ground pork
3/4 cup finely grated Italian bread crumbs
3/4 cup grated imported Romano cheese
3 cloves garlic, minced
3 eggs
1/2 teaspoon salt
1/4 teaspoon black pepper
1/3 cup chopped fresh parsley (or 1 tablespoon dried)
1 tablespoon chopped fresh basil (or 2 teaspoons dried)
Hamburger buns
1 large red onion, sliced
1 large tomato, sliced
4 to 6 lettuce leaves, washed and dried
Marty's Bar-B-Q Sauce

Make a well in the middle of ground meat. Add bread crumbs, cheese, garlic, eggs, spices and herbs, and mix thoroughly to distribute evenly. Separate mixture into 4 or 5 equal parts. Moisten hands and mold meat into patties approximately 3/4- to 1-inch thick. Grill over an open flame, with moistened hickory chips added, until meat is well done (patties should not be pink in the middle).

Serve on grilled hamburger buns with grilled red onions, fresh sliced tomatoes, lettuce, and barbecue sauce. (*Note:* Patties may be made up in advance and either stored in the refrigerator or frozen for up to 3 months.)

Serves 4

WHOLE ROAST PIG

AL BOHNERT

Remember, cook slow! There should be a heavier concentration of charcoal at the shoulder and butt end of the pit to cook pig more evenly.

1 whole pig (90 pounds maximum dressed weight), cleaned and dressed, skin on
1/2 gallon white vinegar
1 ounce crushed red pepper
Barbecue sauce

Twenty-four hours before cooking pig, mix vinegar and pepper.

Split breast bone, approximately first 4 ribs, and hip bone so that pig will lay flat. Place 20 pounds of charcoal in the pit and light. When flame has died, place pig on a grill, split-side down. When charcoal has turned white, arrange coals so that most are underneath the hams and shoulders, with a small amount under the rib cage. When coals begin to die, start additional charcoal outside the pit and add only live coals to the pit. Cook for 4 to 6 hours, depending on size of pig.

When leg joints become stiff, turn pig on its back and continue cooking for 4 to 6 hours more, basting twice with vinegar and pepper mixture. An hour before serving, baste with barbecue sauce. To determine doneness, check hams and shoulders with meat thermometer (temperature should reach 170 degrees before serving).

Serves over 100

LAMB

★ ★ ★ ★

Almost all lamb is more tender than beef or pork and lower in fat and calories. Remove from the grill when the temperature is 5 degrees from desired doneness (the meat continues to cook).

SMOKED STUFFED LEG OF LAMB

KAREN PUTMAN

1 (6- to 7-pound) leg of lamb (about 4 pounds after boning and trimming)
2 large bunches spinach
3 tablespoons olive oil
2 large cloves garlic, minced
1/2 cup fresh bread crumbs
1/4 cup raisins
1/4 cup pine nuts
1/4 cup chopped fresh basil
2 ounces cream cheese
1/2 teaspoon salt
1/4 teaspoon freshly ground black pepper

Bone, trim, and butterfly leg of lamb.

Wash spinach leaves and remove stems, then dry with paper towels. Stack 10 to 12 leaves on top of each other and roll lengthwise, jelly-roll style. Cut crosswise into l/8-inch shreds. Repeat with remaining leaves. Heat olive oil over high heat, then stir in spinach and garlic. Tossing and stirring often, sauté for 2 minutes or until most of the liquid has evaporated.

Spoon spinach mixture into a bowl and stir in bread crumbs, raisins, pine nuts, basil, cheese, salt, and pepper. Spread lamb with spinach mixture and roll up, jelly-roll style, beginning from the long side. With a heavy string, tie rolled lamb at l-inch intervals.

Smoke meat for 5 to 6 hours at low heat over a hickory and apple wood combination. Use a meat thermometer to determine preferred doneness (140 to 170 degrees).

Serves 6–8

SMOKED RACK OF LAMB

RICH DAVIS

1 (8-rib) rack of lamb
1 anchovy fillet
4 cloves garlic, minced
1/2 teaspoon salt
1 teaspoon Dijon mustard
2 teaspoons chopped fresh oregano
4 teaspoons red wine vinegar
1 tablespoon Worcestershire sauce
1/4 teaspoon freshly ground pepper
1/2 cup olive oil
1 cup bread crumbs

Trim excess fat from meat. Combine anchovy, garlic, and salt, and mash to a paste. Add mustard, oregano, vinegar, Worcestershire, and pepper, and slowly whisk in olive oil to incorporate. Rub mixture generously on meat and press bread crumbs into surface. Let stand at room temperature for 30 minutes.

Insert a meat thermometer into center of meat, away from bone. Smoke over indirect heat for approximately 2 hours, until meat thermometer registers preferred doneness.

Serves 3–4

GRILLED LAMB STEAKS WITH MINT SAUCE

2 lean American lamb leg steaks, 1-inch thick
2 tablespoons olive oil
1/4 cup cider vinegar
1/4 cup water
1 tablespoon brown sugar
1 tablespoon black peppercorns, finely crushed
1/3 cup fresh mint leaves, finely chopped

Rub lamb with oil and set aside. Combine vinegar and water, and bring to a boil. Stir in sugar, pepper, and mint, then boil for 3 to 5 minutes to reduce liquid.

Place steaks over hot coals, searing for 2 minutes on each side. Continue grilling for 8 to 10 minutes more, turning and basting with mint sauce until meat reaches desired doneness.

Serves 4–6

BARBECUED LAMB KEBABS

These come from Charlie and Ruthie Knote's Barbecuing & Sausage-Making Secrets *(Culinary Institute of Smoke Cooking, 1993).*

3 pounds lamb, trimmed and cubed
1/2 cup dry red wine
1/4 cup water
1/4 cup canola or vegetable oil
1 tablespoon Worcestershire sauce
1 tablespoon lemon juice

1 teaspoon dry mustard
1/2 teaspoon paprika
1/2 teaspoon granulated garlic or garlic powder
2 teaspoons granulated onion
12 drops Tabasco sauce

Combine lamb with remaining ingredients and marinate for 2 hours at room temperature or overnight in the refrigerator.

Drain lamb and reserve marinade. Skewer meat pieces and grill over a medium-hot fire. Turn and baste with reserved marinade every 3 to 4 minutes until meat reaches desired doneness.

Serves 8

POULTRY

★ ★ ★ ★

The flavors imparted by fruitwoods marry
well with poultry in the smoker. Try different
marinades with this fairly foolproof meat.

"NUCLEAR" CHICKEN WINGS
BOARD ROOM BAR-B-Q

Board Room owner Scott O'Meara advises hosts to serve this appetizer with a generous supply of napkins and cold beverages. These wings won the American Royal Buffalo Wings Contest in 1990.

5 pounds chicken wings (about 60)
1-1/2 cups barbecue spice
3 tablespoons crushed red pepper flakes
1 tablespoon ground red pepper
1 tablespoon chili powder
1 teaspoon black pepper
Barbecue sauce

Cut chicken wings at the first and second joints. Remove tips and discard. Rinse wings and drain. Put spice and peppers in a large paper or plastic bag, add the wings, and shake to coat completely with seasonings. Allow wings to sit for an hour.

Prepare coals, adding a combination of hickory and apple wood chips, and cook wings over an indirect fire for about 1 hour. After an hour, coat wings with barbecue sauce and grill directly over coals, turning constantly, until chicken is browned and done.

Serves 15–20

BARBECUED GIZZARDS
DAVE HALSEY

These are guaranteed to melt in your mouth! You can cook them at the same time you're grilling chicken, filling in the spaces between the pieces of meat with the gizzards.

2 to 3 pounds chicken gizzards
Morton's Nature's Seasons to taste
K.C. Masterpiece barbecue sauce (any label)

Season gizzards with Morton's seasoning. Cook over a low fire (200 to 225 degrees) until tender. Remove gizzards from grill and let soak in a pan of barbecue sauce until ready to serve.

Serves 4–6

BLUE RIBBON BARBECUED CHICKEN
DAVE HALSEY

4 to 6 chicken quarters
Morton's Nature's Seasons to taste
K.C. Masterpiece barbecue sauce (any label)

Prepare coals and let heat for 45 minutes. Season chicken to taste with Morton's seasonings. Cover grill with a single layer of chicken quarters and sear meat for 5 to 7 minutes on each side at 300 degrees. Let fire cool down to 225 degrees, and cook chicken for 1-1/2 hours, turning every 15 minutes. Grill for an additional 20 minutes, basting with barbecue sauce and turning every 5 minutes to keep from burning.

Serves 4–6

DEB'S LIP-LICKIN' CHICKEN
HASTY BAKE OVENS

4 chicken breasts
Seasoned salt to taste
Lemon pepper to taste
Coarsely ground pepper to taste
Minced garlic to taste
1/2 cup soy sauce
1/2 cup Worcestershire sauce

Rinse chicken breasts and pat dry. Rub with spices and minced garlic, then place on a prepared grill bone-side down. Sear for 5 minutes, then turn over and sear for 5 minutes more. Lower firebox to 2/3 down position and, with heat deflector in place, cook for 1 hour and 15 minutes. Put soy sauce and Worcestershire in a spray bottle and use to spray-baste meat frequently (every 20 minutes).

Serves 4–6

WHOLE SMOKED TURKEY

BRUCE "DOC" DANIEL

Whole turkey, rinsed and patted dry
Vegetable oil
Pepper to taste

Rub turkey with oil and sprinkle all over with pepper, including body cavity. Place in a shallow pan over an indirect charcoal fire, using hickory chips soaked in water overnight to create lots of thick, wet smoke.

Bring heat in smoker up to 200 degrees and maintain a steady temperature throughout cooking process. Baste bird every hour with additional oil. Smoke for 45 to 60 minutes per pound. For the final 2 hours of cooking, remove bird from pan and place directly on grill rack.

Servings vary with size of bird

SMOKED TURKEY SALAD
K.C. MASTERPIECE BARBECUE & GRILL

Delicious served on fresh salad greens, in half a cantaloupe, or on good-quality bread as a sandwich filling, this recipe makes plain old chicken salad taste pretty tame.

2-1/4 cups bite-sized pieces of smoked turkey
1 cup chopped red onion
4 hard-boiled eggs, chopped fine
2 cups mayonnaise
2 tablespoons Dijon mustard
1 teaspoon celery salt
1 jalapeño pepper, diced
1 teaspoon white pepper
1 teaspoon black pepper
1 teaspoon ground cumin

Combine turkey, onion, and eggs. In a separate bowl, combine mayonnaise with remaining ingredients. Add mayonnaise mixture to turkey mixture and blend well. Refrigerate until ready to serve.

Serves 6–8

SMOKED DUCK
PEPPERCORN DUCK CLUB, HYATT REGENCY

The hickory chips impart an excellent taste to the duck, which turns a natural golden red.

1 (4- to 4-1/2-pound) duckling
1 teaspoon dried rosemary
1 teaspoon fennel
1 teaspoon anise
1 teaspoon garlic powder
1 teaspoon white pepper
1 teaspoon paprika
1/2 cup salt

Rinse duckling and pat dry. Add herbs and spices to salt and mix well. Rub seasonings all over outside of duck and put 1 tablespoon inside body cavity.

Soak hickory chips in water for at least 30 minutes and sprinkle over prepared coals. Smoke duck on a banked fire away from direct heat for 2-1/2 hours at 200 to 225 degrees. When legs move freely, or when internal temperature in the thigh reaches 160 to 165 degrees, the bird is finished.

Serves 2–4

KANSAS STATE CHAMPIONSHIP CORNISH GAME HENS

DICK MAIS

4 Cornish game hens
2 cups orange juice
3 tablespoons Cointreau
1/4 cup (1/2 stick) butter
1 cup honey
Paprika to taste

Rinse hens and pat dry. Stir orange juice, Cointreau, and butter over low heat until well blended. Using a large bore needle and syringe, inject some orange juice mixture into each side of the breast and thighs of each bird. Add honey to remaining mixture to use as a baste during cooking.

Smoke hens for 4 to 6 hours on a very low grill over mesquite and pecan woods. Thirty minutes before done, sprinkle each with paprika.

Serves 4

FISH & SEAFOOD

★ ★ ★ ★

Unlike meat, marinate fish and seafood
only to impart flavor. Oil the grill rack so
tender flesh won't stick while cooking.

SMOKED TROUT

DICK MAIS

2 (8-ounce) whole trout, cleaned and dressed
1/4 cup salt
2 cups brown sugar
3 cups water
1/2 cup (1 stick) butter
2 tablespoons lemon juice

Soak trout for 8 hours in a mixture of salt, 1 cup brown sugar, and 2 cups water.

Simmer butter, remaining 1 cup brown sugar, 1 cup water, and lemon juice over low heat until well blended. While smoking fish over low heat (using a combination of apple and mesquite woods), baste the inside and skin frequently. If flesh sticks, oil outside of fish and wrap in cheesecloth.

Serves 2

BARBECUED TROUT

CAROLYN WELLS

2 whole trout, cleaned and dressed
2 tablespoons fresh lemon juice, plus additional to brush on fish
2 cups liquid marinade (such as Wicker's Marinade and Baste)
1/2 cup vegetable oil
1/2 teaspoon dried tarragon
1/2 teaspoon dried chervil
2 medium onions, sliced and separated into rings

Split each trout down the middle and brush with lemon juice inside and out. Place fish in a shallow pan. Combine marinade, oil, lemon juice, and seasonings. Arrange onion rings under and on top of fish. Pour marinade over all, cover, and refrigerate for 1 to 2 hours.

Drain off marinade and reserve. Discard onion rings. Cook fish over a bed of hot coals until done (15 to 20 minutes), basting frequently with reserved marinade.

Serves 2

CILANTRO-BUTTERED TROUT WITH TOMATO SALSA

KAREN ADLER

This recipe is from Karen's book, Hooked on Fish on the Grill.

4 whole rainbow trout, cleaned and dressed
2 lemons, sliced
4 sprigs fresh cilantro plus 1 tablespoon chopped
Salt and freshly ground pepper to taste
1/2 cup (1 stick) butter
2 tablespoons lemon juice
Cooked brown rice

In the cavity of each fish, place 2 or 3 slices of lemon and 1 sprig of cilantro. Season with salt and pepper. Melt butter and add lemon juice plus 1 table-spoon chopped cilantro.

Grill trout over hot coals for 6 to 7 minutes per side until meat turns white, basting occasionally with cilantro-butter mixture. Serve with Tomato Salsa and brown rice.

Serves 4

TOMATO SALSA

2 cups chopped ripe tomatoes
1/2 onion, diced
3 banana peppers, diced
1/4 cup Italian dressing
1/4 teaspoon crushed red pepper flakes

Combine all ingredients and refrigerate until ready to serve.

Makes about 3 cups

PRIZE-WINNING SMOKED CATFISH

JESSICA KIRK

1 (4- to 6-pound) whole catfish, cleaned and dressed
Vegetable oil
Salt

Brush oil over catfish and lightly salt. Liberally oil a cheesecloth and tie a knot in the bottom of it. Slip in the catfish, head first, and hang in a smoker tail-end up. Slow-cook for 4 hours at 225 degrees.

Serves 4

PEPPER TUNA

BRENDA BURNS

4 tablespoons pink peppercorns
4 tablespoons green peppercorns
4 (6- to 8-ounce) tuna steaks
1 lemon, cut into wedges

Crush together pink and green peppercorns and use to coat the surface of each tuna steak. Grill fish over hot coals for approximately 2-1/2 minutes per side (tuna will toughen if overcooked). Serve with lemon wedges.

Serves 4

STIR-GRILLED SALMON AND SUGARSNAP PEAS

KAREN ADLER

This is Karen's favorite grill wok recipe from her book, Hooked on Fish on the Grill, *combining texture, color, and taste at its best!*

1 pound salmon steak or fillets, cubed
1/2 pound sugarsnap peas, cleaned and stems removed
12 cherry tomatoes
1/2 red onion, sliced
3 cups cooked white rice

MARINADE
1/4 cup soy sauce
1/4 cup rice wine vinegar
2 tablespoons honey
4 cloves garlic, minced
1 teaspoon ground ginger
1 teaspoon sesame paste (tahini)

Combine marinade ingredients in a glass bowl. Add salmon, peas, tomatoes, and onions, and marinate for 30 minutes or more.

Pour salmon mixture into a well-greased grill wok over the sink and partially drain liquid.

Place wok over hot coals and, using large wooden spoons, stir-grill fish and vegetables for 6 to 8 minutes. Move wok to indirect-heat side of grill, close lid, and cook for 4 to 5 minutes more. Serve with rice.

Serves 4

GRILLED SALMON WITH HORSERADISH SAUCE
SMOKESTACK BAR-B-Q OF MARTIN CITY

Make sure the grill is very hot before cooking, so that the exterior of the salmon is seared and the interior stays moist.

2 teaspoons salt
Pinch of white pepper
Pinch of freshly ground black pepper
4 (8-ounce) salmon fillets

BASTE
2 cups (4 sticks) butter
1/2 teaspoon garlic powder
2 teaspoons minced fresh parsley
2 teaspoons lemon juice

Combine salt and peppers, and sprinkle mixture over salmon fillets. To make baste, melt butter over low heat. Skim off milky foam that forms and chill remainder. When butter has hardened again, transfer to a small saucepan (discarding any sediment) and reheat. Add garlic powder, parsley, and lemon juice, and remove from heat.

Using hickory logs or chips, build a hot fire in the grill. When fire has reached peak temperature, raise rack 8 to 12 inches above flame. Place salmon fillets skin-side up on grill and let sear for about 3 minutes (do not let flame touch fish). Turn carefully, baste with herbed butter and continue to grill, basting several times during cooking. A fillet 3/4-inch thick should need no more than 8 minutes grilling (do not overcook). Serve with Horseradish Sauce on the side.

Serves 4

HORSERADISH SAUCE

2 egg yolks
1 tablespoon lemon juice
1/2 teaspoon dry mustard
1/2 teaspoon Dijon mustard
1/4 teaspoon kosher salt

1/4 teaspoon white pepper
1/2 cup vegetable oil
1/2 cup extra-virgin olive oil
1/3 cup prepared horseradish
2 tablespoons chopped fresh parsley

Thoroughly combine egg yolks, lemon juice, mustards, salt, and white pepper in a blender or food processor. With the motor running, add oils in a slow, steady stream so that mixture will emulsify into mayonnaise. Add horseradish and parsley, and blend briefly. Transfer to a bowl, cover tightly, and refrigerate for at least 2 hours.

Makes about 2 cups

CITRUS-GRILLED ORANGE ROUGHY

Orange roughy fillets are tapered and thin at one end. To avoid overcooking the tapered end, simply fold the tip over.

4 (6- to 8-ounce) orange roughy fillets

MARINADE
1/2 cup olive oil
1/4 cup dry white wine
1 clove garlic, finely chopped
1/2 teaspoon crushed red pepper flakes
1/2 teaspoon chopped fresh parsley
1/4 teaspoon salt
1/4 teaspoon freshly ground pepper
Grated zest of 1 orange
Juice of 1 orange

Combine marinade ingredients and pour over fish in a glass dish. Cover and refrigerate for 30 minutes.

Remove fish from marinade and reserve liquid. Arrange fish, skin-side down, on a grill topper. Grill until fillets flake easily (about 5 minutes per side), basting with remaining marinade while cooking. Serve immediately.

Serves 4

BARBECUED SNAPPER IN CAJUN-STYLE SAUCE
KIKI LUCENTE

4 pounds red snapper or bass

SAUCE
2 medium onions, quartered
3 cloves garlic
2 tablespoons chopped fresh parsley
3/4 teaspoon Louisiana hot sauce
Water
1/4 cup vegetable oil
1-1/2 teaspoons salt
1 cup Sautérne
1 tablespoon lemon juice
3 tablespoons Worcestershire sauce
1 (13-ounce) can tomato sauce

To make sauce, whirl onions, garlic, parsley, and hot sauce in a blender or food processor. Add enough water to blend. Pour mixture into a pan, add oil, and simmer over low heat for about 40 minutes. Add salt, wine, lemon juice, Worcestershire, and tomato sauce. Simmer for about 1 hour more, covered, adding more water if needed.

Place fish on a sheet of heavy foil and cover with sauce. Seal foil and place packet on a prepared grill. Cook covered for 1 hour over a low fire, turning every 20 minutes. Remove fish from foil and place on grill for 10 minutes. Turn and cook for 10 minutes more, basting with sauce.

Serves 6

CHAMPIONSHIP BARBECUED SHRIMP
VINTAGE SWINE TEAM

2 pounds jumbo shrimp, peeled, deveined, and butterflied (tails intact)
1 cup (2 sticks) unsalted butter, melted
1 cup Wicker's Marinade and Baste
3 cloves garlic, minced

SAUCE
1 (13-ounce) can tomato sauce
1 cup Wicker's Marinade and Baste
1/2 cup brown sugar
1 tablespoon lemon juice
2 tablespoons Worcestershire sauce
1 to 2 tablespoons prepared horseradish

Toss shrimp with combined butter, marinade, and garlic, and refrigerate (covered) for several hours.

Combine sauce ingredients and simmer over low heat until sauce mixture is reduced by half. Set aside.

Grill shrimp over hot fire for 3 to 5 minutes (if cooked longer, shrimp will toughen). Serve with sauce on the side.

Serves 3–4

SOUTHERN-STYLE BARBECUED SHRIMP

JIM FLYNN

1/2 cup chopped onion

1/2 cup chopped celery

1 clove garlic, minced

3 tablespoons vegetable oil

1 (16-ounce) can tomatoes, drained and chopped

1 cup K.C. Masterpiece barbecue sauce (original)

1-1/2 teaspoons salt

1 teaspoon white vinegar

1 teaspoon chili powder

1 tablespoon Worcestershire sauce

Dash of Tabasco sauce

1 teaspoon cornstarch

2 teaspoons water

1 pound jumbo shrimp, peeled and deveined

1/2 cup chopped green bell pepper

3 cups cooked rice

Sauté onion, celery, and garlic in hot oil until tender. Add tomatoes, barbecue sauce, salt, vinegar, chili powder, Worcestershire, and Tabasco. Simmer uncovered for 45 minutes.

Mix cornstarch with water and stir into sauce. Cook and stir until mixture thickens. Add shrimp and green pepper. Cover and simmer until shrimp are cooked, about 5 to 10 minutes. Serve over a bed of rice.

Serves 2–3

SAUSAGE

★ ★ ★ ★

Kansas City has many purveyors of fine fresh
sausage (refer to the resource guide), or
you may want to learn to make your own!

CREOLE SMOKED SAUSAGE

PAUL KIRK

If this isn't hot enough for your taste buds, add more red pepper (flakes and ground) a little at a time. Keep the meat as cold as possible when making this sausage.

7 pounds fresh boneless pork
2 large onions, minced
1 clove garlic, crushed
2 tablespoons salt
2 teaspoons black pepper
1 teaspoon crushed red pepper flakes
1 teaspoon paprika
1/2 teaspoon ground red pepper
1 tablespoon dried parsley flakes
1/2 teaspoon ground allspice
1/4 teaspoon powdered bay leaf
1/4 teaspoon ground nutmeg
5 yards sausage casing

Grind pork, using the coarse knife of a meat grinder. Add onions, garlic, and all seasonings, and mix thoroughly. Regrind. Stuff mixture into casings, then refrigerate overnight. Smoke or grill to serve.

Serves 10–12

FAMOUS HOT LINKS SAUSAGE

OTIS BOYD

2-1/2 pounds ground pork shoulder
2-1/2 pounds ground beef (brisket, round, or sirloin)
2 teaspoons rubbed sage
2 teaspoons crushed red pepper flakes
2 teaspoons paprika
2 teaspoons ground cumin
2 teaspoons dried basil
2 teaspoons anise seeds
2 teaspoons dried oregano
Dash of salt and black pepper
Sausage casings (optional)

Combine meats and spices. For links, fill casings with meat mixture to desired length, cut casings, and secure ends with string. Barbecue at 225 degrees for 2 hours or slow smoke for 4 hours at 185 degrees. For patties, form mixture into a roll and cover with waxed paper. Carve patties from the roll and peel off waxed paper. Patties can be fried or grilled.

Serves 8–10

BARBECUED SAUSAGE

GUY SIMPSON AND MARVIN DAVIS

4 teaspoons salt
4 teaspoons sugar
3 teaspoons rubbed sage
1 teaspoon ground nutmeg
2 teaspoons ground pepper

1/2 cup hot water
4 pounds pork butts, coarsely ground
8 feet sausage casings

Combine seasonings with hot water. Pour mixture into meat and work it in by hand. Stuff mixture into casings. Barbecue over low heat (225 degrees) for 2-1/2 hours, turning once. (Use indirect heat for best results.)

Serves 8

BARBECUED SAUSAGE BALLS
RUTH DAVIS

1 pound bulk sausage
1 beaten egg
1/3 cup bread crumbs
1/2 teaspoon rubbed sage

SAUCE
1/2 cup K.C. Masterpiece barbecue sauce (hickory flavored)
2 tablespoons brown sugar
1 tablespoon white vinegar
1 tablespoon soy sauce

Combine sausage with egg, bread crumbs, and sage, and form into small balls. Brown in an ungreased skillet, then pour off fat. Combine sauce ingredients, pour over sausage balls, and heat for 20 minutes over low heat.

Serves 6–8

BRATWURST WITH MUSTARD SAUCE
KAREN ADLER

4 (12-ounce) bratwurst links
4 toasted garlic buns

SAUCE
1/4 cup (1/2 stick) butter
1/4 cup firmly packed light brown sugar
1 tablespoon dry mustard
1 tablespoon lemon juice

To make sauce, melt butter and add brown sugar, mustard, and lemon juice. Keep warm. Cut three slits in each bratwurst, then place slit-sides down on a hot grill. Grill for 4 to 6 minutes, then turn. Spoon a teaspoon of sauce into each slit. Grill for 3 to 4 minutes more, until evenly browned. Serve on buns with remaining sauce.

Serves 4

GAME

★ ★ ★ ★

Venison or elk may be substituted in many
beef recipes. Cook to medium-rare for best
results (game toughens if overcooked).

VENISON RIBS

CAROLYN WELLS

Side of venison ribs
1 bottle Wicker's Marinade and Baste

MARINADE
1/2 cup vegetable oil
1/4 cup white vinegar
1/4 cup chopped onion
1 teaspoon salt
2 teaspoons Worcestershire sauce
1 liter Lambrusco

Place ribs in a covered pan, add combined marinade ingredients, and marinate for 4 days in the refrigerator, turning twice a day.

Drain off marinade and place ribs on a prepared grill. Baste with Wicker's and cook for 4 hours over low heat (200 degrees), continuing to baste occasionally with additional Wicker's.

Serves 4

VENISON CHOPS

KAREN ADLER

8 venison chops (deer or elk)

MARINADE
1/2 cup red wine
1/4 cup light soy sauce
1/4 cup honey
2 tablespoons chopped fresh basil
2 cloves garlic, minced

Combine marinade ingredients and marinate chops in the refrigerator for 2 to 4 hours.

Grill over medium-hot coals for 4 to 6 minutes per side.

Serves 4

PRIZE-WINNING BARBECUED VENISON

DAVE HALSEY

1 (3-pound) venison roast
Morton's Nature's Seasons to taste
K.C. Masterpiece barbecue sauce (original)

MARINADE
3/4 cup red wine vinegar
3/4 cup vegetable oil
3/4 cup ketchup
3 tablespoons Worcestershire sauce
1-1/2 tablespoons garlic salt
1-1/2 teaspoons dry mustard
Dash of pepper

Season meat with Morton's seasoning. Combine marinade ingredients, cover roast with mixture, and marinate overnight in the refrigerator.

Remove roast and reserve marinade. Prepare coals around sides of the grill and allow to cook down for 45 minutes. To seal meat, put roast in the center of the hot grill (covered) for 30 minutes, turning every 5 minutes to prevent drying out. Let roast cook for 1-1/2 hours more at 225 degrees, turning every 15 to 20 minutes and basting occasionally with reserved marinade. Cook for 30 minutes more, basting frequently with barbecue sauce and continuing to turn every 5 minutes so meat doesn't burn.

Serves 4–6

ELK STEAK WITH FRESH HERB MARINADE

KAREN ADLER

1-1/2 to 2 pounds elk sirloin

MARINADE
3/4 cup olive oil
1/4 cup white vinegar
2 cloves garlic, minced
2 teaspoons chopped fresh oregano
2 teaspoons chopped fresh basil
2 teaspoons chopped fresh rosemary
Salt and pepper to taste

Combine marinade ingredients and marinate elk in refrigerator overnight.
Remove meat and reserve marinade. Prepare a medium fire. Grill elk over direct heat for 10 to 12 minutes, turning once and basting with reserved marinade. (Adjust cooking time to temperature of grill; elk is very lean and toughens if overcooked.)

Serves 6–8

BUFFALO'S BARBECUED SQUIRREL

JOHN F. (BUFFALO) GATTENBY

1 squirrel or rabbit, dressed, washed, and patted dry
1 cup Heinz 57 sauce
1 cup honey

Prepare fresh meat immediately. Smoke at 200 degrees in an aluminum tray (using a mixture of hickory, cherry, and apple woods, soaked in water overnight), basting continually with pan juices until meat is tender (at least 1 to 2 hours). Glaze with a mixture of Heinz 57 and honey 20 minutes before removing meat from the grill.

Serves 2

Rubs, Marinades, & Sauces

Liquid marinades and sauces keep in the refrigerator for up to 1 week, or in the freezer for 2 to 3 months. Dry rubs hold longer.

COWTOWN COOKERS' BASIC BARBECUE RUB

JOHN SCHLOSSER

2 cups sugar
1-1/2 cups barbecue spice
3/4 cups salt
1/2 cup seasoned salt
1/2 teaspoons garlic powder
1/2 teaspoon paprika
1/2 teaspoon ground red pepper
1 tablespoon mustard seed

Combine all ingredients and mix well. Sprinkle generously on meat and rub it in. Let sit at least 30 minutes before cooking.

Makes about 5 cups

BASIC DRY RUB

RICH DAVIS

Feel free to experiment—omit the salt, cut ingredients in half, or add seasoned garlic, celery, or onion salts. Keep trying until you get a combination that works for you.

1/2 cup brown sugar
1/2 cup coarsely ground black pepper
1/2 cup paprika
1/4 cup chili powder
1/4 cup salt
2 tablespoons garlic powder

Combine ingredients well and rub into meat before barbecuing.

Makes about 2 cups

BASIC BARBECUE RUB
PAUL KIRK

2 cups sugar
1 cup barbecue spice
1/2 cup salt

Combine ingredients and blend well. Rub heavily on meat before barbecuing.

Makes 3-1/2 cups

TEXAS BARBECUE RUB
PAUL KIRK

1 cup salt
1 cup black pepper
1 cup paprika

Combine ingredients thoroughly and rub on meat before barbecuing.

Makes 3 cups

SAVORY POULTRY RUB
KAREN ADLER

1 tablespoon garlic powder
2 tablespoons dried tarragon
1 tablespoon poultry seasoning
2 tablespoons lemon pepper
1 tablespoon paprika
2 teaspoons salt

Combine all ingredients and rub into meat before cooking.

Makes 1/2 cup

HERB MIX FOR FISH

The longer the coating remains on fish, the more pungent the flavor.

4 teaspoons dried lemon peel
3 teaspoons dried tarragon
3 teaspoons dried chervil
2-1/2 teaspoons garlic powder
2-1/2 teaspoons freshly ground pepper
3/4 teaspoon salt
1/2 teaspoon crushed red pepper flakes

Combine all ingredients. Lightly oil fish before coating; use about 1 teaspoon of mixture per serving. Keeps in a tightly covered glass jar for several weeks.

Makes about 1/3 cup

BLACKENED SEASONING
SHIFRA STEIN

2 teaspoons lemon pepper marinade
1 teaspoon garlic powder
1 tablespoon paprika
1 teaspoon dried parsley flakes
1 teaspoon dried basil
1/2 teaspoon freshly ground pepper
1/2 teaspoon ground red pepper
1/2 teaspoon salt

Combine all ingredients. Sprinkle 1/2 to 1 teaspoon of mix on a lightly oiled fillet of red snapper, catfish, tuna, or other fish of your choice. Keeps in a tightly covered glass jar for several weeks.

Makes about 1/4 cup

SOUTHERN-STYLE VINEGAR MARINADE AND BASTE
DICK MAIS

This mixture also acts as a natural tenderizer.

2 cups cider vinegar
1 cup K.C. Masterpiece barbecue sauce (original)
2 tablespoons lemon juice
1 tablespoon dry mustard

Combine ingredients and simmer mixture over low heat until well blended. Cool. Cover meat and marinate for up to 24 hours in the refrigerator.

Makes about 3 cups

CHICKEN AND FISH MARINADE AND BASTE
DICK MAIS

2 tablespoons Dijon mustard
2 tablespoons lemon juice
1/2 cup (1 stick) butter
1 teaspoon Lawry's seasoned salt

Combine ingredients and simmer mixture over low heat for 10 minutes. Cover chicken or fish and marinate for 30 minutes in the refrigerator. Use remaining liquid as a baste.

Makes about 2/3 cup

CHINESE BBQ SAUCE

RICH DAVIS

3/4 cup K.C. Masterpiece barbecue sauce (original)
2 tablespoons soy sauce
1 tablespoon cider vinegar
1 tablespoon peanut oil
1/2 teaspoon fresh anise seed, ground
1/2 teaspoon ground ginger
1/2 teaspoon minced garlic

Combine ingredients and simmer for 5 minutes. Serve with barbecued ribs or chicken. (Recipe may be doubled; keeps 2 to 3 weeks in a covered glass jar in the refrigerator.)

Makes about 1 cup

HERBED BARBECUE SAUCE

JEANNE BUNN

1/4 cup chopped onion
2 tablespoons vegetable oil
2 cups ketchup
1/3 cup honey
1/4 cup Worcestershire sauce
1 teaspoon prepared horseradish
   mustard
1/2 teaspoon liquid smoke
1 teaspoon white vinegar
1/4 teaspoon garlic salt
1/4 teaspoon coarsely-cracked pepper
1/4 teaspoon crushed dried rosemary

1/4 teaspoon crushed dried thyme
1/4 teaspoon crushed dried oregano
1/4 teaspoon crushed dried savory
2 drops Tabasco sauce

Sauté onion in oil until tender. Add remaining ingredients and simmer, uncovered, for 10 to 15 minutes.

Makes about 3 cups

COWTOWN COOKERS' BASIC BARBECUE SAUCE

JOHN SCHLOSSER

1 (32-ounce) bottle ketchup
1 cup dark molasses
1-1/2 tablespoons Tabasco sauce
1-1/2 medium onions, chopped fine
1 large green bell pepper, chopped fine
1/2 cup lemon juice
1 teaspoon garlic powder
2-1/2 tablespoons dry mustard
3 tablespoons white vinegar
3/4 cup brown sugar
1/4 cup liquid smoke
1/4 cup Worcestershire sauce

Combine all ingredients in a large pot. Rinse out ketchup bottle with 1/4 cup water and pour into pot. Bring mixture to a boil, stirring constantly. Reduce heat and simmer until onion and peppers are tender (about 2 hours).

Makes about 6 cups

TANGY BARBECUE SAUCE

ART JACKSON

1 (32-ounce) bottle ketchup
1/3 cup sugar
1 (8-ounce) jar barbecue seasoning spice
1 (32-ounce) bottle vinegar
1 teaspoon black pepper
6 tablespoons A-1 Steak Sauce
6 tablespoons Worcestershire sauce

Thoroughly combine ketchup, sugar, and barbecue seasoning, then add vinegar, pepper, and A-1 and Worcestershire sauces. Stir until mixed well. Simmer over medium heat for 5 minutes (optional) and serve.

Makes about 1/2 gallon

STEPHENSON'S BARBECUE SAUCE
STEVE STEPHENSON

2 (14-ounce) bottles ketchup
3 tablespoons prepared horseradish
3 tablespoons salad mustard
2 tablespoons Worcestershire sauce
1 tablespoon lemon juice
1 teaspoon celery seed
1/4 teaspoon onion salt
1/4 teaspoon ground red pepper
1/4 teaspoon liquid smoke
1/4 teaspoon garlic juice

Blend together all ingredients and refrigerate in a covered glass jar. Heat and serve with meat.

Makes about 4 cups

THE BARON'S STEAK SAUCE
PAUL KIRK

1/2 pound beef suet (fat trimmings from brisket or steak)
1/2 cup (1 stick) butter
1 cup fresh mushrooms, sliced thin
1 clove garlic, minced
1/2 cup dry white wine
2 tablespoons A-1 steak sauce
1 tablespoon Worcestershire sauce

Place suet in a large skillet and heat until 1/4 cup of grease is rendered. Remove any remaining suet, then add butter, mushrooms, and garlic. Sauté until mushrooms are soft, then stir in remaining ingredients. Reduce heat and simmer for 15 minutes or until mixture starts to thicken. Serve with steaks.

Makes about 3-1/2 cups

ACCOMPANIMENTS

★ ★ ★ ★

To fix side dishes on the grill, surround
the pan with heavy-duty foil, tightly seal,
and prick a couple of holes in the top.

EASY MELON SALAD

RICH DAVIS

1 cantaloupe
1 honeydew melon
1 large slice watermelon
1 (8-ounce) bottle Wishbone Italian dressing
6 ounces crumbled Stilton or other blue cheese

Make 20 to 30 melon balls from cantaloupe. Repeat with honeydew and watermelon to yield 6 cups melon balls. Place in a large bowl with dressing and cheese. Stir gently. Chill and serve as a salad or appetizer.

Serves 8–10

BLACK-EYED PEA SALAD

RICH DAVIS

3 (15-ounce) cans black-eyed peas, rinsed and drained
1/2 cup diced green bell pepper
1/2 cup chopped onion
1/3 cup cider vinegar
1/4 cup dark molasses
2 tablespoons peanut oil
1-1/2 teaspoons salt
1-1/2 teaspoons ground cumin
1 teaspoon garlic powder
1 teaspoon Worcestershire sauce
1/2 teaspoon dry mustard
1/4 teaspoon black pepper
1/4 teaspoon Tabasco sauce

Combine peas, green pepper, and onion. In a separate bowl, combine remaining ingredients. Pour over vegetables and stir gently to coat. Chill and serve cold.

Serves 8–10

MARINATED GREEN BEAN SALAD
STEPHENSON'S APPLE TREE INN

2/3 cup vegetable oil
1/3 cup white wine vinegar
1/2 teaspoon salt
1/4 teaspoon onion salt
1/4 teaspoon seasoned salt
1/4 teaspoon dry mustard
2 pounds fresh green beans, blanched until crisp-tender (or two 16-ounce
   cans green beans, drained)

Mix oil, vinegar, and seasonings together, and pour over beans, mixing lightly.
Cover and chill overnight.

Serves 8

CREAMY DIJON POTATO SALAD
RICH DAVIS

9 medium potatoes
4 hard-cooked egg whites, chopped
2/3 cup finely chopped dill pickle
1/2 cup finely chopped celery
1/3 cup finely chopped onion
2 cups Hellman's reduced-fat mayonnaise
2 tablespoons Dijon mustard
2 teaspoons salt
1 teaspoon paprika
1 teaspoon finely ground black pepper
1 teaspoon Lawry's seasoned salt

Boil potatoes until tender, then peel and cube to yield 9 cups. Combine potatoes with egg whites, dill pickle, celery and onion. Combine remaining ingredients and add to potato mixture, tossing gently. Refrigerate until serving time.

Serves 14–16

CREOLE POTATO SALAD

PAUL KIRK

5 pounds red potatoes
1/4 cup vegetable oil
1/4 cup white vinegar
1 medium onion, finely chopped
6 stalks celery, finely chopped
6 green onions, finely sliced
1 tablespoon minced fresh parsley
6 hard-boiled eggs, mashed fine
1/4 teaspoon Louisiana hot sauce
Pinch of powdered thyme
1/4 teaspoon salt
1/4 teaspoon white pepper
2 chicken bouillon cubes
2 tablespoons water
1 cup mayonnaise or salad dressing

Boil potatoes until soft. Drain and cool, then peel and cut to desired size. Place in a bowl, pour in oil and vinegar, and mix well. Add onions, celery, green onions, parsley, and eggs. Mix gently. Add hot sauce, thyme, salt, and pepper. Combine bouillon cubes and water and simmer until cubes melt. Pour bouillon mixture over salad and toss gently. Add mayonnaise and mix again.

Serves 10–12

BAYOU HOT SLAW

PAUL KIRK

To crank up the heat, add more red pepper.

1 medium head cabbage (2-1/2 to 3 pounds), shredded and chopped
1 large onion, minced
1 large green bell pepper, minced
1 small red bell pepper, minced
4 stalks celery, thinly sliced
1/2 cup Wesson oil
1 bay leaf
2 tablespoons all-purpose flour
1/2 cup sugar
1 cup water
1-1/4 cups white vinegar
1 teaspoon Worcestershire sauce
1/2 teaspoon white pepper
1/2 teaspoon dry mustard
1/2 teaspoon granulated garlic
1/4 teaspoon ground red pepper

Combine vegetables in a large salad bowl and mix well. Heat oil and bay leaf, then stir in flour (don't let it brown). Add sugar and water, stirring until mixture thickens. Pour in vinegar and remaining ingredients, stirring until mixture becomes a smooth, thick sauce. Cool almost completely before pouring over slaw vegetables. Toss and mix well. Chill and serve cold.

Serves 6

COUNTRY COLESLAW

VIRGINIA GREGORY

1 medium head cabbage, shredded (8 cups)
1 to 2 medium onions, diced (2 cups)
3 tablespoons chopped canned pimento, drained
6 tablespoons chopped green bell pepper
3/4 cup white vinegar
1 cup sugar
1/2 teaspoon celery salt
1 heaping tablespoon salt
1 teaspoon celery seed
Salt to taste

Combine all ingredients except salt, blend well, and barely cover with boiling water. Let stand for 1 hour. Pack into jars and refrigerate overnight. Drain and salt lightly before serving.

Serves 6

COLESLAW WITH BOILED DRESSING

RICH DAVIS

1/2 teaspoon celery salt
1/4 teaspoon garlic salt
1 teaspoon dry mustard
1/8 teaspoon black pepper
1/4 teaspoon salt
1/4 teaspoon paprika

2 tablespoons sugar
1/2 cup water
1 egg
1/3 cup cider vinegar
4 cups shredded cabbage

Dissolve celery salt, garlic salt, dry mustard, pepper, salt, paprika, and sugar in water. Beat egg lightly in a small, heavy saucepan. Place over low heat and immediately beat in vinegar and dissolved spice mixture, stirring constantly until mixture thickens (about 5 minutes). Chill. Pour over shredded cabbage and toss well.

Serves 3–4

MARTY'S BAR-B-Q HOUSE DRESSING

This salad dressing also makes a good marinade or baste for meat, fish, or poultry. For a sweeter variation, add sugar to taste (about 1/2 to 1 teaspoon).

2 cups Marty's Bar-B-Q Sauce
1 cup Italian dressing

Shake ingredients in a covered jar until mixed thoroughly. Serve over mixed greens or a combination salad. (May be used immediately after mixing and/or stored in the refrigerator for up to 1 month.)

Makes 3 cups

DEVILISHLY GOOD BARBECUED EGGS

RICH DAVIS

4 hard-boiled eggs
1/4 teaspoon salt
2 tablespoons K.C. Masterpiece barbecue sauce (original)
2 tablespoons mayonnaise
2 teaspoons finely minced dill pickle
Finely chopped fresh parsley, to garnish

Slice eggs in half lengthwise. Remove yolks and mash, then add salt, barbecue sauce, mayonnaise, and dill pickle. Mix well with a fork and stuff egg halves with mixture. Sprinkle with chopped parsley, chill, and serve.

Serves 4–8

BANDALERO BAKED BEANS

DICK MAIS

1 (16-ounce) can pork-and-beans
1 (16-ounce) can pinto beans
1 (16-ounce) can red kidney beans
1 (16-ounce) can butter beans
1 (16-ounce) can navy or Great Northern beans
1 cup chopped onion
1 cup K.C. Masterpiece barbecue sauce (original)
1 cup chopped smoked sausage (or barbecued beef or pork)
1 tablespoon liquid smoke (optional)

Combine all ingredients and bake at 325 degrees for 1-1/2 hours. If using left-over barbecue for meat base, do not use liquid smoke.

Serves 14–16

BARBECUED BEANS

STEVE STEPHENSON

2 (16-ounce) cans pork-and-beans
1 (15-ounce) can tomatoes, drained
1 cup apple cider
1/2 cup ketchup
1/2 cup brown sugar
1/2 onion, chopped
2 tablespoons prepared horseradish
1 tablespoon Worcestershire sauce
1 teaspoon seasoned salt
1 teaspoon dry mustard
1/2 teaspoon pepper
1/4 teaspoon Accent or MSG (optional)

Mix all ingredients in a shallow 3-quart baking dish. Bake at 350 degrees for 1-1/2 to 2 hours.

Serves 6–8

INDIAN-STYLE BAKED BEANS

JUDITH EPSTEIN

If the barbecue sauce you use is spicy, you may want to cut down on the chili powder here. If the sauce is smoky, you might want to use less liquid smoke. Taste as you go along and see what happens.

3/4 pound bacon
2 large (40-ounce) cans pork-and-beans
1/2 cup brown sugar
2 tablespoons minced onion
2 tablespoons chili powder
2 tablespoons prepared mustard
2 teaspoons liquid smoke
1 cup barbecue sauce
1/2 cup dark Karo syrup
1/2 cup molasses

Fry bacon until almost done and drain on paper towels. When cool, tear into small pieces. Drain off a little of the liquid from canned beans, discard the little pieces of pork fat, and combine beans with bacon and all other ingredients. Bake covered at 325 degrees for an hour and 15 minutes, or in a Crockpot for 6 or 7 hours on the low setting.

Serves 12–14

BARBECUED BAKED BEANS

RICH DAVIS

2 (16-ounce) cans pork-and-beans, drained
3/4 cup K.C. Masterpiece barbecue sauce (original)
1/2 cup brown sugar
1 teaspoon ground cumin
1/2 teaspoon ground red pepper
1 tart apple, peeled, seeded, and chopped (Jonathan or Granny Smith)
1 ounce golden raisins
1 medium onion, chopped
3 strips uncooked bacon, cut in half (or substitute 2 tablespoons butter)

Preheat oven to 350 degrees. Combine all ingredients except bacon in a
2-quart baking dish. Top with bacon (or dots of butter) and bake uncovered
for 1 hour.

Serves 6–8

PIT-BAKED BEANS

SNEAD'S CORNER BAR-B-Q

4 cups canned pork-and-beans
1/2 cup brown sugar
1/2 large onion, minced
1/4 cup Heinz ketchup
1 cup Snead's Mild Barbecue sauce
1/3 cup Snead's Hot Barbecue sauce
2 tablespoons prepared mustard
Bacon or chopped smoked meat to taste
Salt and pepper to taste

Combine all ingredients in a heavy covered baking dish. To cook beans in the
oven, bake for at least 1 hour at 350 degrees. To use the grill, soak hickory
chips in water, then spread over hot coals. Close the grill and cook beans over
low heat for several hours.

Serves 6–8

FRESH VEGETABLE KABOBS
SMOKESTACK BAR-B-QUE OF MARTIN CITY

2 cups (4 sticks) butter (or light olive oil)
1/2 teaspoon garlic powder
1 teaspoon minced fresh parsley
2 teaspoons lemon juice
2 small onions, peeled
4 (1-1/2-inch) carrot slices, cut diagonally, blanched for 3 minutes
4 (2-inch) pieces fresh corn on the cob
4 (1/2-inch) slices zucchini, cut diagonally
4 (1/2-inch) slices yellow squash, cut diagonally
4 large mushroom caps
8 (2-inch-square) pieces green bell pepper
Salt and freshly ground pepper to taste

Soak 4 (12-inch) wooden skewers in water for 30 minutes (or use flat metal skewers). Melt butter over low heat. Skim off foam, then slowly pour clear yellow liquid into another container (discard milky residue). Add garlic powder, parsley, and lemon juice to clarified butter. Set aside.

Wash vegetables and thread onto skewers, starting and ending with green pepper, and brush with butter mixture. Grill over a hot hickory fire. (For a gas grill, enclose soaked hickory chips in a foil packet. Poke holes in packet and place on briquets.) Baste with additional butter mixture while grilling. Turn often and cook until vegetables are lightly browned but still firm. Season and serve.

Serves 4

BARBECUED ONIONS
SHIFRA STEIN

1 large peeled white onion per person
Olive oil
Granulated garlic
Tarragon
Salt and pepper

Place each onion on an individual square of aluminum foil. Rub onions generously with olive oil, then sprinkle with garlic, tarragon, salt, and pepper. Seal foil around onions and cook directly over coals for about 30 minutes. Serve in foil jackets.

Servings vary

OUTDOOR BAKED ONION SURPRISE
RICH DAVIS

You can be foolproof creative and try various fillings with these onions.

6 large, flat-bottomed onions
6 tablespoons butter
3 teaspoons Lawry's seasoned salt (or oregano and sweet basil)

Trim off outer layers until onions are shiny and smooth. Cut off onion top and core out center about 1 inch deep. Fill center of each onion with 1 tablespoon butter and 1/2 teaspoon seasoned salt (or stuff with oregano, sweet basil, and butter). Grease individual squares of aluminum foil and wrap each onion tightly. Place in a 300-degree hot barbecue oven and bake for 45 to 50 minutes.

Serves 6

FRIED CORN
JASON STEIN

1/4 cup (1/2 stick) butter or margarine
2 cans niblet yellow corn, drained thoroughly
2 jalapeños, chopped (optional)
1 tablespoon McCormick Salad Supreme (optional)
Salt and pepper to taste

Melt butter in a heavy skillet and fry corn and jalapeños together until brown. Add seasonings to taste. When done, corn should be hot and chewy.

Serves 4

CHEESY CORN BAKE
SMOKESTACK BAR-B-Q OF MARTIN CITY

2 tablespoons butter
2 tablespoons all-purpose flour
1/2 teaspoon dry mustard
1 to 1-1/2 cups hot milk (plus additional, if necessary)
2/3 cup grated Cheddar cheese
2 (3-ounce) packages cream cheese, cut into pieces
3 ounces smoked ham, diced (about 1/3 cup)
2 teaspoons garlic salt
1-1/4 cups milk
4 cups frozen corn kernels (don't thaw)

Melt butter in a small, heavy saucepan, add flour, and cook over low heat for 2 minutes, stirring to blend (do not let mixture brown). Mix in mustard, then milk, and stir to incorporate. Simmer over low heat until thickened. Stir in Cheddar and blend well. Add more milk if mixture is too thick.

Preheat oven to 325 degrees. Combine cheese sauce with cream cheese, ham, garlic salt, and milk in a 2-quart casserole. Bake until cream cheese melts, about 20 minutes. Remove from oven and stir. Add frozen corn, mix again, and bake for 30 minutes more. Serve immediately.

Serves 4

SWADDLED CORN ON THE COB

DICK MAIS

6 ears fresh corn
1 cup milk
1/2 cup (1 stick) butter
Salt and pepper to taste

Shuck and clean corn. Soak 12 paper towels in milk. Spread butter over corn and season with salt and pepper. Wrap corn in milk-soaked towels (2 towels per piece), and then wrap each ear in foil. Place on a moderate grill for 45 minutes (do not place directly over fire).

Serves 6

AVERY ISLAND POTATO PANCAKES

LINDSAY SHANNON

6 medium red potatoes, peeled
1/2 cup (1 stick) butter, plus additional for frying
Milk or half-and-half
1/2 cup all-purpose flour, plus additional
2 medium onions, grated (optional)
Salt and pepper to taste
2 fresh eggs
3 to 5 drops Louisiana hot sauce or Tabasco sauce

Boil potatoes until tender. Drain and mash potatoes, adding butter, milk, flour, onion, salt, and pepper a little at a time. Taste, then add more butter, milk, salt, or pepper if needed. Refrigerate.

   Combine eggs and hot sauce. Once potato mixture is cold, mold into pancake shapes, dip in egg–hot sauce mixture, and dust with additional flour. Grease a cast iron skillet with butter and fry pancakes until both sides have a crust.

Serves 4

MOLLY POTTS DIRTY RICE

PAUL KIRK

1/4 cup Wesson oil
2 cups Uncle Ben's long-grain rice
1 bay leaf
1 quart water
1 green bell pepper, diced
1 red bell pepper, diced
4 stalks celery, sliced
1 small onion, minced
1/2 small tomato, diced
1 clove garlic, crushed
1 teaspoon Worcestershire sauce
1 teaspoon crushed red pepper flakes
1/2 teaspoon dry mustard
1/2 teaspoon white pepper
1/4 teaspoon ground cumin
2 chicken bouillon cubes
1/2 pound ground beef, browned and seasoned with salt and pepper to taste

Place oil in a 3-quart saucepan and heat until hot. Add rice and bay leaf, stir, and sauté until rice turns light brown. Add remaining ingredients except for ground beef, bring to a boil, and stir well to dissolve bouillon. Cover with a tight-fitting lid and turn off heat. Let sit undisturbed on the burner for 30 minutes or longer. Fold seasoned beef into rice mixture and serve hot.

Serves 8

CRIMSON SAUERKRAUT

SERENA HAMMER

2 (27-ounce) cans sauerkraut, including liquid
1-1/2 (10-1/4-ounce) cans condensed tomato soup
Enough water to rinse can
1/2 cup brown sugar
3 tablespoons schmaltz (rendered chicken fat) or melted butter
Sugar to taste

Combine all ingredients well and spoon into a greased 3-quart casserole. Bake, uncovered, at 350 degrees for 30 minutes. Lower heat to 300 degrees and bake for 60 to 90 minutes more. Toward the end of baking time, stir in a small amount of sugar to taste.

Serves 10–12

ANN'S SPICY JALAPEÑO CORNBREAD

1 package cornbread mix
2 eggs
1 cup water
1 jalapeño, finely chopped
1 (4-ounce) can green chiles, chopped
1 (8-3/4-ounce) can creamed corn
3 tablespoons chopped onion
4 ounces grated Cheddar cheese
1 teaspoon chili powder (optional)

Preheat oven to 425 degrees. Grease a 9-inch square baking pan. Combine all ingredients, pour batter into prepared pan, and bake for 40 minutes. Serve warm or at room temperature.

Serves 6–8

DESSERTS

★ ★ ★ ★

Summer fruits, cool ice creams,
and old-fashioned cakes make perfect
endings to a spicy, smoky meal.

CHERRY CRISP
SHIFRA STEIN

1/4 cup low-fat sour cream
3 tablespoons plus 1 teaspoon light brown sugar
4 cups pitted fresh sweet cherries
1/2 cup all-purpose flour
2 tablespoons sugar
2 tablespoons margarine

Thoroughly combine sour cream and 1 tablespoon plus 1 teaspoon brown sugar. Cover and chill for at least 30 minutes.

Place cherries in an 8-inch square baking pan and set aside. Combine flour, sugar, remaining 2 tablespoons brown sugar, and margarine until crumbly. Sprinkle over cherries. Bake at 375 degrees for 40 minutes or until lightly browned. Top individual portions with sour cream mixture and serve.

Serves 6

HOMEMADE VANILLA ICE CREAM
KAREN ADLER

3/4 cup sugar
2 tablespoons all-purpose flour
2 eggs, beaten
2 cups milk
2 cups heavy cream
1 tablespoon vanilla extract

Combine sugar and flour in a heavy saucepan. Stir in eggs and milk, then bring just to a boil over medium heat. Remove from heat and let cool. Stir in cream and vanilla, then chill mixture thoroughly. Transfer mixture to an ice cream maker and follow manufacturer's instructions.

Makes 1 quart

CHOCOLATE PEANUT BUTTER ICE CREAM PIE

K.C. MASTERPIECE BARBECUE & GRILL

15 chocolate sandwich cookies
1/2 cup dry-roasted peanuts
1/4 cup (1/2 stick) butter or margarine, melted
3 quarts chocolate ice cream
7 (1.8-ounce) chocolate-covered peanut butter cups
1 cup heavy cream
2 tablespoons sugar
1 (8-ounce) jar milk chocolate fudge topping
1/4 cup strong coffee
2 tablespoons coffee-flavored liqueur

Preheat oven to 400 degrees. In a food processor, finely chop together cookies and peanuts. Set aside 1 tablespoon of mixture for garnish. Spray a 9-inch pie pan with vegetable cooking spray. In pie pan, mix together butter and remaining cookie mixture by hand. Press mixture onto bottom and up sides of pan. Bake for 8 minutes, then cool on a wire rack.

Remove ice cream from freezer and place in refrigerator for about 40 minutes to soften slightly. Coarsely chop peanut butter cups. Gently mix softened ice cream with chopped peanut butter cups and spoon into cooled cookie crust. Freeze until firm (overnight).

Beat heavy cream and sugar until stiff peaks form. Spoon whipped cream into decorating bag and pipe rosettes on outside edge of pie and on top. Sprinkle reserved cookie crumb mixture on top of pie. Place pie in freezer, but do not cover until whipped cream has hardened.

To serve, let pie stand at room temperature for 15 minutes for easier slicing. Over low heat, heat fudge topping until hot, then stir in coffee and coffee liqueur until blended. Serve slices of pie topped with warm fudge sauce.

Serves 8–12

HICKORY NUT PIE
STEPHENSON'S APPLE TREE INN

When folks talk hickory in Kansas City, they usually mean hickory logs used for barbecue smokers. But hickory nuts, native to this area, are also tasty. Substitute pecans here if you prefer.

2 tablespoons all-purpose flour
1 tablespoon sugar
3 eggs
1/3 cup milk
1-1/2 teaspoons vanilla extract
1 (16-ounce) bottle light corn syrup
1-1/2 teaspoons butter
2 tablespoons graham cracker crumbs
1 cup shelled hickory nuts (or pecans)
1 (9-inch) unbaked pie shell
Whipped cream and chopped hickory nuts to garnish

Mix flour and sugar, then beat in eggs, milk, and vanilla until smooth. Bring syrup and butter to a boil over low heat. Remove from heat and beat syrup into egg mixture, whisking constantly. Set aside.

Sprinkle graham cracker crumbs and nuts over bottom of pie shell, then pour filling into shell. Bake at 325 degrees for 45 minutes or until filling has just set firmly. Cool before serving. Mound each slice with whipped cream and sprinkle with chopped nuts before serving.

Serves 8–10

SWEET POTATO PIES

MARILYN MOORE

3-1/2 pounds fresh sweet potatoes
1 cup (2 sticks) butter or margarine, plus additional to rub on sweet
  potatoes
1/2 cup milk
4 large eggs
1-1/2 cups sugar
1/2 cup all-purpose flour
1 tablespoon baking powder
1 tablespoon ground nutmeg
2 teaspoons ground cinnamon
4 (8-inch) deep dish unbaked pie shells

Wash sweet potatoes, pat dry, and rub with butter. Cover sweet potatoes with water, bring to a boil, then reduce heat and simmer until soft. Drain and cool potatoes.

Preheat oven to 350 degrees. Peel potatoes and cut into 1/4-inch slices across the grain. Melt butter, add milk, eggs, and sugar, mix well, and add to sweet potatoes. Sift flour, baking powder, nutmeg, and cinnamon, then stir into sweet potato mixture. Pour into uncooked pie shells. Bake for 40 minutes or until filling is firm.

Serves a crowd

PEANUT BUTTER CUSTARD CAKE

PAUL KIRK

2 packages plain gelatin
3/4 cup orange juice
1 cup crunchy peanut butter
1/4 cup all-purpose flour
1 cup plus 3 tablespoons sugar
1/4 teaspoon salt
2 cups half-and-half
3 eggs, separated
1 angel food cake (hard and stale)
1 cup heavy cream, whipped
1/2 cup roasted Georgia peanuts, chopped

Dissolve gelatin in orange juice. In a double boiler, cook peanut butter, flour, 1 cup sugar, salt, and half-and-half, stirring until well blended and thickened. While hot, stir in gelatin mixture and egg yolks. Remove from heat and cool.

Beat egg whites until stiff, then add remaining 3 tablespoons sugar. Fold into cooled custard. Break cake into bite-sized pieces, and layer with custard in a greased mold or angel food cake pan. Refrigerate overnight.

Unmold cake, top with whipped cream, and garnish with chopped peanuts to serve.

Serves 8–10

SAUERKRAUT SOUR CREAM SPICE CAKE
PAUL KIRK

2 cups brown sugar
1/2 cup vegetable shortening
3 large eggs
2 cups sauerkraut, drained and chopped fine
2 teaspoons ground cloves
2 teaspoons ground cinnamon
2 teaspoons ground allspice
1/4 teaspoon salt
2-1/2 cups all-purpose flour
1 teaspoon baking soda
1-1/4 cups sour cream

ICING
1 cup firmly packed brown sugar
1/2 cup (1 stick) butter, room temperature
1/4 cup heavy or light cream
1 cup chopped pecans

Preheat oven to 375 degrees. Cream sugar and shortening. Beat in eggs one at a time. Add sauerkraut, spices, and salt, blending well. Add flour, baking soda, and sour cream, alternately mixing. Pour batter into a greased, 10-by-15 inch cake pan and bake for approximately 30 to 45 minutes.

To make icing, cream together sugar and butter. Add cream a little at a time until mixture is smooth. Spread over warm cake and top with pecans. Place under the broiler until icing starts to bubble.

Serves 10–15

SWEET POTATO PONE IN EARLY TIMES SAUCE
LINDSAY SHANNON

3 cups grated raw sweet potatoes
1/2 cup sugar
1/4 cup unbleached all-purpose flour
2 eggs
1/2 cup dark molasses
1/2 to 1-1/2 teaspoons ground nutmeg, to taste
1 teaspoon vanilla extract
1/4 cup (1/2 stick) butter, melted

SAUCE
1/2 cup (1 stick) butter
1 egg
1 cup sugar
1/2 cup Early Times bourbon (only Kentucky bourbon will do)

Preheat oven to 350 degrees. Combine sweet potatoes, sugar, flour, eggs, molasses, nutmeg, and vanilla, then stir melted butter into mixture. Pour mixture into a cast iron skillet and bake for about 50 minutes.

To make sauce, cut butter into small pieces and melt in a double boiler over hot water. Mix egg and sugar, and add to melted butter. Stir with a wooden spoon until sugar dissolves completely and egg is cooked (about 2 minutes). Don't let sauce boil. Remove from heat, allow sauce to cool to room temperature, and then slowly mix in bourbon. Slice sweet potato pone and serve drizzled with sauce.

Serves 8

THUNDER THIGHS' INDIAN BREAD PUDDING

1 loaf bakery-style egg bread, sliced
2 cups sugar
3 cups very hot water
1 teaspoon vanilla extract
2 teaspoons ground cinnamon
1/2 cup (1 stick) butter
2 cups raisins
1 pound grated mild Cheddar or longhorn cheese
Cream (optional)

Toast bread lightly and cut off crusts. Butter one side of slices and place buttered side down in a greased 9-by-13-inch glass baking dish. Make 2 layers of bread in the pan.

Pour sugar into a heavy, deep saucepan over medium-high heat, stirring constantly until sugar melts and becomes a dark caramel color (about 8 minutes). Remove from heat and, taking care to protect against splattering, slowly pour hot water in a slow stream into melted sugar. (At first sugar will sizzle and harden into lumps, but it will dissolve as mixture is stirred.) Keep stirring over medium-low heat until all dissolves, then add vanilla and cinnamon, simmering for 1 to 2 minutes.

Preheat oven to 350 degrees. Sprinkle raisins over bread, then sprinkle grated cheese over raisins. Carefully pour sugar syrup over all, making sure that all the cheese is moistened with syrup. Bake for 30 minutes (don't overcook!), then serve warm topped with cream if desired.

Serves 12

BLACK WALNUT BOURBON BROWNIES

KAREN ADLER

This is a rich, moist, dense brownie.

6 tablespoons butter
3 ounces semisweet chocolate
2 ounces usweetened chocolate
1 large egg
1 cup sugar
1/4 teaspoon salt
1 teaspoon vanilla extract
2 tablespoons bourbon
1/2 cup all-purpose flour
1/2 cup black walnut pieces

Melt butter in a heavy saucepan, the add chocolate and melt (take care not to burn). Set aside to cool.

Preheat oven to 350 degrees. Beat egg until lemon-colored and frothy. Beat in sugar and salt. Add chocolate mixture, vanilla, and bourbon. Stir in flour and nuts. Spread batter evenly in a greased 8-inch square baking pan. Bake for 20 to 25 minutes, or until a toothpick inserted in the center comes out clean (do not overbake).

Serves 6–8

CHOCOLATE BARS WITH COCONUT ICING

DEE CONDE

2 cups all-purpose flour
2 cups sugar
1/2 teaspoon salt
1/2 cup (1 stick) margarine
1/2 cup Wesson oil
1/4 cup cocoa
1 cup water
2 eggs
1/2 cup buttermilk
1 teaspoon baking soda
1 teaspoon vanilla extract

ICING
1/2 cup (1 stick) margarine
1/4 cup cocoa
1/3 cup buttermilk
1 pound confectioners' sugar
1/2 cup shredded coconut
1/2 cup chopped nuts

Preheat oven to 400 degrees. Sift together flour, sugar, and salt. Set aside. Combine margarine, oil, cocoa, and water, and bring to a boil. Pour over flour mixture and blend. Combine eggs, buttermilk, baking soda, and vanilla, and stir into batter mixture. Pour into a greased and floured jelly-roll pan and bake for 20 minutes.

To make icing, combine margarine, cocoa, and buttermilk, and bring to a boil. Remove from heat and blend in confectioners' sugar, then add coconut and nuts. Spread on cooled bars.

Serves 12–15

CHOCOLATE TURTLE BARS

MARY ANN DUCKERS

1 (14-ounce) package caramels
2/3 cup evaporated milk
1 package German chocolate cake mix
3/4 cup (1-1/2 sticks) butter, melted
1 cup chopped pecans
1 cup semisweet chocolate chips

In a double boiler, melt caramels with 1/3 cup milk, stirring constantly. Set aside.

Preheat oven to 350 degrees. Combine cake mix, melted butter, and remaining 1/3 cup of milk. Blend until mixture holds together. Press half of dough into a greased and floured 9-by-13-inch baking pan. Bake for 6 minutes, then remove and sprinkle pecans and nuts and chocolate chips over crust. Spread caramel mixture over pecans and nuts and chocolate chips, then crumble remaining dough over caramel layer. Bake for 15 to 18 minutes more. Cool and refrigerate until caramel sets, then cut into bars and serve.

Makes about 20 bars

RESTAURANTS

★ ★ ★ ★

**Just a "taste" of the over 90 barbecue
restaurants in Kansas City**

★ RESTAURANTS ★

Many thanks to Remus Powers, Ph.B., for permission to use excerpts from his Kansas City BBQ Pocket Guide *(Pig Out Publications, 1992).*

B. B.'S LAWNSIDE BAR-B-Q
1205 E. 85th Street, Kansas City, MO 64131; (816)822-7427
Cash. Dine in/carry out.

Lindsay Shannon's love for blues and BBQ creates the perfect blend at this roadhouse. Great barbecue with a Southern flair (try the barbecued gumbo) plus live blues and jazz make this a choice stop on weekends.

BOARD ROOM BAR B-Q
9600 Antioch Road, Overland Park, KS 66212; (913)642-6273
Cash. Dine in/carry out.

Chief Executive Pitmaster Scott O'Meara invites your investment in a stock that's easy on the pocketbook and pays high dividends in taste and stress reduction. "Escape from the corporate bull" and head to the Boardroom.

BOYD 'N SONS BARBECUE
5510 Prospect Avenue, Kansas City, MO 64130; (816)523-0436
Cash. Dine in/carry out. Sauce bottled for sale.

Mr. Otis Boyd, master chef and renowned pitmaster, serves up barbecue that has earned the rating "As Good As We've Ever Had" from *Real Barbecue* authors Greg Johnson and Vince Staten. Be sure to try the smoked lamb and sausage along with the basics.

ARTHUR BRYANT BARBEQUE
1727 Brooklyn, Kansas City, MO 64127; (816)231-1123
Cash. Cafeteria-style dine-in/carry out. Sauce bottled for sale.

This Kansas City landmark is steeped in myth, legend, and hype, having been called "world class," "the choice of presidents," and "Mecca" by thousands of barbecue aficionados. It was described by Calvin Trillin as "the single best restaurant in the world."

GATES BAR-B-Q
4707 The Paseo, Kansas City, MO 64110; (816)923-0900
2001 W. 103rd Terrace, Overland Park, KS 66206; (913)383-1752
1026 State Avenue, Kansas City, KS 66102; (913)621-1134

1411 Swope Parkway, Kansas City, MO 64110; (816)921-0409
1221 Brooklyn Avenue, Kansas City, MO 64127; (816)483-3880
10440 E. 40 Highway, Kansas City, MO 64055; (816)353-5880
215 N. Rawhide Drive, Olathe, KS 66062; (913)764-6210
Cash. Dine in/carry out. Sauce bottled for sale.

Ollie Gates has Kansas City covered. A barbecue legend, he serves up some of the most popular 'que known to man. Everything's made from scratch here. The tangy potato salad is a winner, and save room for the sweet potato pie. Gates sauce won "Best Barbecue Sauce on the Planet" in the 1991 American Royal International Barbecue Sauce competition.

HAYWARD'S PIT BAR-B-QUE
11051 Antioch Road, Overland Park, KS 66210; (913)451-8080
Cash/credit cards. Dine in/carry out. Sauce bottled for sale.

Hayward Spears continues in the tradition of Arthur Bryant. This family-run operation serves delicious sausage, ribs, and lamb. Located in suburban Johnson County, the restaurant is modern with attractive touches of glass, brick and wood paneling, but the barbecue is a traditional pit-smoked slice of heaven.

K.C. MASTERPIECE BARBECUE & GRILL
10985 Metcalf Avenue, Overland Park, KS 66210; (913)345-1199
4747 Wyandotte Street, Kansas City, MO 64112; (816)531-3332
611 N. Lindbergh, Creve Coeur, MO 63141; (314)991-5811
16123 S. Chesterfield Parkway, Chesterfield, MO 63017; (314)530-0052
100 N. McHenry Road, Buffalo Grove, IL 60089; (708)459-1124
1400 Butterfield Road, Downers Grove, IL 60515; (708)889-1999
Cash/credit cards. Dine in/carry out. Sauce bottled for sale.

These upscale eateries belonging to Rich Davis and family offer extensive choices, including Kansas City–style ribs and brisket, North Carolina pork sandwiches, and sinful desserts like Cinnamon Pear Cake with Whiskey Sauce.

KEEGAN'S BAR-B-Q
325 E. 135th Street, Martin City, MO 64145; (816)942-7550
Cash/credit cards. Dine in/carry out. Sauce bottled for sale.

Tim Keegan is religious about his mission to smoke the best barbecue in the world for you. When you step into his place you could get confused about whether you've entered a storefront gospel house or a barbecue restaurant. Sit down and order up . . . and the confusion is over!

LIL' JAKE'S EAT IT & BEAT IT
1227 Grand Avenue, Kansas City, MO 64106; (816)283-0880
Cash. Counter service/carry out. Sauce bottled for sale.

Lil' Jake's is small in size, monumental in taste, and a living Kansas City treasure. Danny Edwards and his pit crew are serious about one thing, preparing and serving good barbecue. Go. Eat. Leave. Go again.

MARTY'S BAR-B-Q
2516 N.E. Vivion Road, Kansas City, MO 64118; (816)453-2222
Cash/credit cards. Dine in/carry out/catering/custom smoking. Sauce bottled for sale.

Everything's good here, and there's so much to choose from, but the beef brisket, burnt ends, pork spareribs, baby back ribs, and turkey are outstanding. True to her taste for foods with an Italian accent, Jean Tamburello offers an excellent marinated coleslaw laced with Italian seasonings.

PORKY'S PIT BAR-B-Q
4728 Parallel Parkway, Kansas City, KS 66104; (913)287-9688
Cash. Counter service/carry out. Sauce bottled for sale.

Porky's sits proudly as a purveyor of quality barbecue in what appears to be a converted drive-in restaurant. After tasting Porky's tender, smoky, fall-off-the-bones pork spareribs, you'll be converted, too.

ROSEDALE BARBEQUE
600 Southwest Boulevard, Kansas City, KS 66103; (913)262-0343
Cash. Dine in/carry out. Sauce bottled for sale.

Slather your ribs and beef here with the famous Rosedale sauce, which has inspired at least a dozen other local sauces. This is one of the "must visit" barbecue institutions of Kansas City.

SMOKE STACK BAR-B-Q OF MARTIN CITY (JACK FIORELLA'S)
13441 Holmes Road, Martin City, MO 64145; (816)942-9141
Cash/credit cards. Dine in/carry out. Sauce bottled for sale.

Smoke Stack features barbecue that isn't easy to find in KC—beef ribs, baby Denver lamb ribs, and fabulous fresh smoked fish. Side dishes worth cheering for are the salads, fresh coleslaw, cheesy corn bake, onion rings, and some of the best pit beans in town. The interior of the restaurant is cozy and Victorian with rooms that wind all over.

SNEAD'S CORNER BAR-B-Q
801 E. 171st Street, Belton, MO 64012; (816)331-9858
Cash/credit cards. Dine in/carry out. Sauce bottled for sale.

Turkey, ham, pork, beef, burnt ends called "brownies," and ribs have attracted tens of thousands of hungry customers to this hilltop barbecue beacon for almost four decades. You'll understand why Alan Richman, a writer for *People* magazine, put Snead's in America's Top 10 barbecue restaurants.

STEPHENSON'S OLD APPLE FARM
40 Highway and Old Lee's Summit Road, Kansas City, MO 64136;
  (816)373-5400
STEPHENSON'S APPLE TREE INN
5755 N.W. Northwood Road, Kansas City, MO 64151; (816)587-9300
Cash/credit cards. Dine in/carry out. Sauce bottled for sale.

These are not barbecue restaurants per se, but here apple and hickory woods are utilized in a closed pit to smoke brisket of beef, pork chops, chicken, ribs, and gizzards that are superb. Top off your meal with fresh baked apple fritters or hot apple pie with brandy sauce. Savor Stephenson's style of home cooking and gracious country dining.

WINSLOW'S CITY MARKET SMOKEHOUSE
20 E. 5th Street, Kansas City, MO 64106; (816)471-RIBS
Cash/credit cards. Dine in/carry out. Sauce bottled for sale.

For taste and value you can't beat the beef sandwich here—the meat is lean, with a beautiful smoke ring and just the right touch of smoke. Winslow's sauce perfectly complements their meat. After your meal stick around and enjoy some good 'ol blues.

ZARDA BAR-B-Q
11931 W. 87th Street, Lenexa, KS 66215; (913)492-2330
214 N. 7 Highway, Blue Springs, MO 64015; (816)229-9999
Cash/credit cards. Dine in/carry out. Sauce bottled for sale.

Great beef and pork combo sandwiches, burnt ends, and ribs are tops here. Throw in Zarda's excellent beans, an order of onion rings, and a bottle of Zarda's classic Kansas City sauce, and you've got the makings of memorable 'que.

SOURCE GUIDE

★ ★ ★ ★

**All the makings of Kansas City barbecue —
meats, sauces, woods, contests, and more**

★ MEATS AND SAUSAGE ★

This listing identifies many independently owned retail meat markets and purveyors of meat gift packages. Kansas City also boasts numerous fine chain supermarkets with in-store full-line sausage kitchens.

BICHELMEYER'S
706 Cheyenne, Kansas City, KS; (913)342-5945
2307 Troost, Kansas City, MO 64108; (816)471-6328

The Bichelmeyer brothers are second generation meat processors. Jim and John hold down the Cheyenne store; Jerry is at the Troost location. Homemade sausages, sides of beef, party pigs, half hogs, chicken, and fish make up just a few of one's choices at Bichelmeyer's. The Troost location is home of the K.C. Sizzler Sausage, a unique tasty blend of spicy barbecue seasonings concocted by Jerry. Also, try the new Buttermilk Sausage—either throw some links on the grill for a great outdoor breakfast, or add some of the bulk variety to ground beef for a flavorful burger.

BOYLE MEAT COMPANY
500 E. 3rd Street, Kansas City, MO 64106; (816)842-5852

Boyle's Famous Corned Beef is a Kansas City institution. This company also ships gift boxes of KC strip steaks, filets, rib eyes, and T-bones. A tasty hickory-smoked ham and ready-to-eat hen turkey are other specialty offerings.

FRITZ'S SMOKED MEAT PRODUCTS
10326 State Line Road, Leawood, KS 66206; (913)381-4618

The Plapp family has been processing and smoking fine meats here since 1927. Sample their barbecue chicken, turkey breast, beef brisket, and pork ribs, or choose several sausages from more than 30 that they make. Their smoked bacon is delicious, too. The Plapps also offer custom smoking of USDA-inspected meats. Try the private label Fritz's Bar B.Q. Sauce in a 16-ounce jar.

HOLIDAY HAM COMPANY
11548 W. 95th Street, Overland Park, KS 66214; (913)894-0222

This attractive retail shop specializes in honey-glazed hams, but other delicious offerings include smoked whole turkeys and turkey breast. Send a gift of KC strip steaks or filet mignons. The smoked pork tenderloin is great served cold, or you can heat it up on your grill in less than five minutes.

KANSAS CITY STEAK COMPANY
3501 Guinotte Avenue, Kansas City, MO 64120; (800)524-1844

Steaks reign supreme at this company—premium Angus beef filets, KC strips, steak burgers, rib eyes, prime rib roasts, T-bones, Chateaubriand, and Porterhouse. The weight and size of steaks ranges from 3/4-inch thick for a filet to a hefty 1-1/2-inch, 16-ounce strip. Orders are gift-packed in dry ice to assure perfect delivery.

KRIZMAN'S HOUSE OF SAUSAGE
424 N. 6th Street, Kansas City, KS 66101; (913)371-3185

Started by Joe Krizman, Sr., in 1939, this operation remains a family affair with Joe Jr., Joe III, and nephew Jack continuing the tradition. Krizman's is probably the largest supplier of specialty sausage to the restaurant industry in town. If you've tasted the great sausages at Hayward's, Smokestack, Johnny's, and Arthur Bryant's, you've tasted Krizman's. Run, don't walk, here for a barbecue sausage fix.

McGONIGLES FOOD STORE
1307 W. 79th Street, Kansas City, MO 64114; (816)444-4720

This charming neighborhood grocery is known for its top-quality meat counter. Mike McGonigle's family has owned this full-service store since 1951. They custom butcher to customers' specifications, and specialty items include buffalo, rabbit, pheasant, quail, venison, and free-range chicken. They also ship nationwide.

NORTH OAK QUALITY MEAT MARKET
7711 North Oak Trafficway, Kansas City, MO 64118; (816)436-1602

Judy and Dan Zager have owned this shop for over 20 years. They proudly sponsor Bill and Wendy Rabon's KC's Three Alarm Smokers competitive barbecue team. Judy says they're known for their choice aged corn-fed beef, fresh whole chickens, beef briskets, spareribs, and baby back ribs.

SCIMECA'S THRIFTWAY
1447 Independence Avenue, Kansas City, MO 64117; (816)842-6387

If you want Italian sausage, here it is. Founded May 13, 1935, by Phil Scimeca's grandfather, this is the oldest independent retail grocer in the city. Standard Italian fare plus harder-to-find items like capacolla and proscuitto ham, pancetta, and several types of Genoa salami are top grade here. Try the Italian olive salad—it's great with barbecued and grilled foods.

STEVE'S MEAT MARKET
32685 Lexington, DeSoto, KS 66018; (913)583-1390

Owner Steve Pruden is proud of his market's Kill Creek Barbecue Sauce, which comes in sweet, tangy, and hot. It's nicknamed the "sauce's boss." Known for excellent Polish sausage, Steve also sells his top-grade meats to several competitive barbecuers.

WERNER'S SPECIALTY FOODS
5736 Johnson Drive, Mission, KS 66202; (913)362-5955

This skilled butcher from Germany has learned the American way with meat from packinghouse to point-of-purchase. At Swanson's in Westport, Werner added some Swedish and Norwegian to his repertoire and makes just about the best Norwegian potato sausage you'll find. His meat counter offers top-grade meats. Shop on Saturdays and order one of his sausages hot off the grill. This is bratwurst heaven.

WILEY'S COUNTRY BOY MEAT COMPANY
101 E. Gilman Road, Lansing KS 66043; (913)262-5245

Owners Dan and Mary Ann Stewart says the best way to describe this business is that it's an old-fashioned meat market. Anything you want, they have. As you walk into the retail store, you feast your eyes on gargantuan amounts of meat. There's a second room in back that has again as much . . . maybe over 60,000 pounds on display. If you order a 1-inch T-bone steak, it's likely to be cut from a huge side of beef while you watch. Customers include one of the past Grand Champions of the American Royal Barbecue Contest.

WINTERS MEAT PROCESSING PLANT
110 N. 12th Street, Blue Springs, MO 64015; (816)229-3151

The Winter family, with mother Berta and sons Perry and Jack, has been running this operation since 1967. They butcher and process all choice and prime beef and hogs. Their specialties include party pigs, whole hogs, and turkey sausage. Meats are slow-smoked over hickory sawdust.

★ SAUCES AND SEASONINGS ★

The flavor of most barbecued meats, fish, and fowl can be enhanced by season-ings and sauces, and Kansas City is blessed to have so many. One could test a different sauce, rub, or marinade every weekend for a year and not experience all that's available locally. Many barbecuers have developed their own secret blends and packaged them for resale. Most of the products listed are available at specialty/gourmet stores and some groceries, as well as by mail order. National brands are not included, except for ones originating in the Kansas City area.

ADRIAN'S BARBECUE SAUCE, INC.
P.O. Box 19261, Lenexa, KS 66219; (913)491-5104

This line includes Adrian's Original, Citrus, Cajun, and Jalapeño. A newcomer to the market, Adrian's has made a big splash in the Midwest. They describe themselves as "a legend in the making."

CHEF DAN'S INC.
10103 Johnson Drive, Merriam, KS 66203
Distributed through Pisciotta's (816)221-6670 and MBC Foods (816)921-3500

Chef Dan's Wild & Spicy and Mild barbecue sauces are a tangy blend of tomato, onion, green pepper, brown sugar, and honey (the onion and green pepper are sautéed in olive oil). Both have won "People's Choice" at the American Royal International Barbecue Sauce Contest. Chef Dan's BBQ Seasoning (a blend of spices with salt, sugar, and turbinado sugar) has won "Tastemaster's Choice" at the Royal; it's great on steaks, chops, and any grilled or barbecued meats.

FLOWER OF THE FLAMES
14406 W. 100th Street, Lenexa, KS 66215; (913)492-1414

Flower of the Flames Raspberry Barbecue Sauce, Original Barbecue Sauce, Honey & Spice Barbecue Sauce, Barbecue Salsa, Dry Rub, Poultry Marinade, and Candise's Kids Que make up this line. The flower herself, Chef Karen Put-man, has won hundreds of awards in barbecue competitions using these prod-ucts. Her raspberry barbecue sauce is particularly popular.

FRITZ'S BAR B Q SAUCE
10326 State Line Road, Leawood, KS 66206; (913)381-4618

Available at Fritz's Smoked Meats, this sauce is the perfect complement to the proprietors' wonderful smoked meats.

GARDEN COMPLEMENTS
1700 Guinotte, Kansas City, MO 64120; (816)421-1090

This outfit manufactures and sells to the trade the following: Old Southern Barbecue Sauce (Traditional, Hickory Smoked, Hearty & Spicy), Aussie Barbecue Sauce, and Aussie Marinade (for Beef & Pork, for Poultry with Herbs, for Poultry with Kiwi Fruit, and for Seafood & Shrimp).

GATES BAR-B-Q INC.
4047 The Paseo, Kansas City, MO; (816)923-0900

Gates Bar-B-Q sauces are well known for their many varieties and availability at area groceries, specialty shops, and Gates Bar-B-Q restaurants. Try the three-pack gift box that contains three varieties of sauce.

GRANDMA RICHIE'S KITCHEN, INC.
(816)761-4222

Jazzy Barbecue Sauce is Carmen Sharp's grandmother's secret barbecue sauce recipe. Carmen will sell her sauce by mail order (call for ordering instructions), but it's also available in local grocery stores and specialty shops.

HAPPY "HOLLA" BAR-B-Q
P.O. Box 822, Shawnee Mission, KS 66201; (913)268-7828

Happy "Holla" BBQ Sauce is somewhat sweet and spicy, the Extra Spicy BBQ Sauce has a little extra bite, and the Hot BBQ Sauce is for those that like it HOT! One taste of the Regular BBQ Salsa and you're hooked; the Hot Salsa has the same great taste, but fiery!

HEARTLAND BAR-B-QUE SAUCE
2450 Grand Ave., Kansas City, MO 64108

The fine sauce served at the Heartland Bar-B-Q in Crown Center is available next door at Blue Ribbon Gourmet. It's also in the Heartland Market Three Pack—a wonderful gift item.

K.C. BARON OF BARBECUE SAUCES
3625 W. 50th Terrace, Roeland Park, KS 66205; (913)262-6029

The "Baron's" line includes K.C. Baron of Barbecue Original Barbecue Sauce, Nice & Spicy Barbecue Sauce, Fire & Smoke Barbecue Sauce, Seasoning & Dry Rub, Barbecue Relish, and Barbecue Salsa. Paul Kirk is the winner of seven world championships and over 375 awards.

K.C. MASTERPIECE BARBECUE SAUCES

Dr. Rich Davis originated these sauces (six flavors in all), which are available nationwide in groceries and are used at the popular K.C. Masterpiece Barbecue & Grill restaurants. In 1990 K.C. Masterpiece sauces won all four first-place award categories in the American Royal Barbecue Sauce Contest.

K.C. RIB DOCTOR
14004 W. 69th Street, Shawnee, KS 66215; (913)268-6115

Guy Simpson, a veteran competitor, uses his Rib Doctor's Rub to season ribs to perfection. Now you can, too.

K-CASS BAR-B-QUE FOOD PRODUCTS
Route 5, Box 336, Pleasant Hill, MO 64080; (816)540-3703

K-Cass Original Bar-B-Que Sauce is a Kansas City–style sauce with a sweet spicy blend of special seasonings that give it an extra kick. The hot variety has a lot of extra kick.

MARTY'S BAR-B-Q
2516 N.E. Vivion Road, Kansas City, MO 64118; (816)453-2222

Marty's Original Classic Bar-B-Q Sauces contain no fat or cholesterol. The Tangy K.C. Style is lightly spiced; the K.C. Style Dijon has a light, mustardy flavor. The Fire Sauce leaves a slow burn, and the Honey Sweet 'n Mild is mildly sweet. Marty's has won several awards in the American Royal International Barbecue Sauce Contest. These sauces are featured at Marty's Bar-B-Q and Marty's Pit Stop.

PISCIOTTA'S, INC.
217 E. Missouri, Kansas City, MO 64106; (816)221-6670

Lots of spices, charcoal, foil, parsley, buffalo steaks, alligator sausage, whole pheasant—stop here for all your barbecue needs.

PLANTER'S SEED AND SPICE COMPANY
513 Walnut Street, Kansas City, MO 64106 (816)842-3651

This City Market institution is a great place to replenish your spice supply. Spices are available in bulk and for home use.

SAUCEMASTER'S GOURMET FOODS, INC.
1105 Westport Road, Kansas City, MO 64111; (816)561-7717

Old K.C. Barbeque Sauce comes in Original and Honey Sweet varieties. There's also Barbeque Spice. These Kansas City–style sauces are a blend of highest quality all-natural ingredients (no MSG or preservatives), and they're great on all barbecued meats.

SPECIALTY SAUCES
(800) SAUCES1 (728-2371)

This out-of-state company specializes in the barbecue sauces of the top pits in the country. Order up a five-pack gift box of Arthur Bryant's Original Barbeque Sauce, McClard's Bar-B-Q (Hot Springs, Arkansas), Charlie Robinson's #1 Rib Restaurant (Chicago), John Wills Bar-B-Que Bar and Grill (Memphis), and Sonny Bryan's (Dallas). Take a national barbecue dine-around in the comfort of your own home.

ZARDA BAR-B-Q AND CATERING CO., INC.
217 N. 7 Highway, Blue Springs, MO 64014; (816)229-9999

Zarda's Bar-B-Q sauces come in Original and Mild varieties. These true Kansas City–style sauces are available at most groceries and are used at the Zarda barbecue restaurants. Zarda also prepares baked beans "just like grandma used to make—thick and rich—the perfect complement to any occasion." The sauces are a rich, zesty blend of over 24 ingredients.

★ GIFTS, GRILLS, AND ACCESSORIES ★

Numerous barbecue-related shopping options cover the Kansas City metropolitan area. Besides the specialty stores, many hardware stores and national chain department stores carry barbecue grills and accessories. Several of the city's hotel gift shops carry an assortment of barbecue products, as do the airport gift shops.

BEST OF KANSAS CITY
6233 Brookside Plaza, Kansas City, MO 64113; (816)333-7900
Crown Center, 2450 Grand Avenue, Kansas City, MO 64108; (816)842-0200

Owner Karen Nash opened her first retail store in the Brookside area in 1982 and has been featuring fine products made in Kansas City ever since. Plenty of barbecue items are on hand, from sauces and seasonings to books, aprons, and grilling gift packs. The Best of Kansas City Barbeque Three Pack is a popular gift box of sauces. Custom gift baskets are a signature here, so go whole hog and order one of their bountiful assortments.

BLUE RIBBON GOURMET
Heartland Market/Crown Center Shops, 2450 Grand Avenue, Kansas City,
**   MO 64108; (816)426-1175**

Kansas City barbecue is king at this shop. Selections include grilling and barbecue cookbooks, clever cow aprons, sauces, spices, grill racks, stove-top smokers, heat-resistant mitts, flavored wood chips (mesquite, hickory, apple, and cherry), custom-made gift baskets—everything but the grill! Heartland Bar-B-Que Sauce can be purchased alone or in the Heartland Market Three Pack along with other barbecue sauces of your choosing.

COCKRELL GENERAL STORE
30003 E. Old 50 Highway, Lee's Summit, MO 64086; (816)697-3611

The aroma of freshly ground coffee invites you into this charming old-fashioned store. Owners Cheri and Kelly Morris stock their shelves with gourmet products and plenty of herb and barbecue seasonings to satisfy the grill enthusiast. Sauces from Jardine's include Killer Bar-B-Q Sauce, Margarita Border-Q Sauce, Chik-n-Lik'n Mustard Base BBQ Sauce, and a mustard that makes a great baste—Bronco Mesquite/Jalapeño Whole Grain Mustard. Closed on Mondays.

COMPLETE HOME CONCEPTS
705 S.E. Melody Lane, Lee's Summit, MO 64063; (816)524-4450
234 N.E. Barry Road, North Kansas City, MO 64155; (816)468-0888

1038 Merriam Lane, Kansas City, KS 66103; (913)831-4172
7214 W. 119th Street, Rosanna Square, Overland Park, KS 66210;
  (913)469-0233

Just like the name says, this store has it all. Owner Jim Goodwin carries several gas grills, an assortment of barbecue tools and accessories, and the Traeger wood smoker, which circulates smoke and heat with an electric fan. The wood source for the Traeger are compressed wood pellets that come in hickory, apple, etc.

EXCLUSIVELY MISSOURI
4621 Shrank Drive, Independence, MO 64055; (816)373-5767

Be ready to browse—this unique store is located in an antique mall. Owner Donna Leker searches the state for gourmet and gift products manufactured in Missouri. Her more unusual barbecue samplings include Mo's Mix and Missouri Classic Sauce from Rolla, Raspberry Summer Sauce from Lampe, and flavorful Vidalia Onion Bar-B-Que Sauce manufactured in DeWitt.

FIREPLACE & BAR-B-Q CENTER
10470 Metcalf Avenue, Overland Park, KS 66212; (813)383-2286
6257 North Oak Trafficway, Kansas City, MO 64118; (816)453-5500

An extensive selection of charcoal and gas grills await you at these stores. Owner Steve Sweet also keeps a well-versed staff on hand to answer all of your barbecuing questions. Wood chips and chunks plus plenty of grill accessories and replacement parts are available here. Ask about their amazing 7-in-1 Smoker.

HALLS
Crown Center, 200 E. 25th Street, Kansas City, MO 64108; (816)274-8100
Country Club Plaza, 211 Nichols Road, Kansas City, MO 64112;
  (816)274-3222

These stores are owned by Hallmark Cards, Inc., whose slogan "When you care enough to send the very best" applies to Halls' barbecue offerings as well. Here you can get the Cadillac of barbecue rigs, the Hasty Bake Oven, which features a moveable grill grid and temperature gauge, plus a separate fire door and drawer easy enough for a novice to operate. (Halls takes special orders for this grill at their Plaza location.) Check out the Kansas City barbecue sauces, grill books, and summer dinnerware, too.

HOT STUFF FIREPLACE & PATIO
9220 Marshall Drive, Lenexa, KS 66215; (913)894-4747

Husband and wife team Bruce and Linda Larison own this fine shop, where you'll find Broilmaster, TEC, and Pro Chef gas grills along with barbecue tools and grill parts. For the weekend barbecuer they offer the most popular sizes of the Oklahoma Joe Smokers (14-inch, 16-inch Tradition, and the 20-inch Chuck Wagon). Bruce and Linda stock sauces and spices from Oklahoma Joe and Adrian's of Kansas City, plus this is the place to get apple, cherry, and hickory chunk woods or wood chips in just about any flavor you want.

KANSAS SAMPLER

9548 Antioch Road, Overland Park, KS 66212; (913)383-2920
Mission Center, 4751 Johnson Drive, Mission, KS 66205; (913)432-3355
Best Western Hallmark Inn, 7000 W. 108th Street, Overland Park, KS 66211;
  (913)385-0099
1801 S. Wanamaker A-7, Topeka, KS 66604; (913)272-9080
State Fair Sampler, 1820 Market, St. Louis, MO 63103; (314)241-8664

Don't let the name deceive you—there are ample products here from Missouri, too. Owner/founder Peg Leibert stocks gourmet foods from both states, with plenty of barbecue finds from which to choose. A wide assortment of sauces, spices, rubs, books, aprons, relishes, woods, and smoker kits can be purchased separately or gathered into a custom-prepared Kansas or Missouri sampler box, mailable wherever your heart desires.

LOUISBURG CIDER MILL

Route 2, W. Highway 68, Louisburg, KS 66053; (913)837-5202

Always bustlin' during apple pickin' time, the Sherman family has taken their wonderful cider mill to even tastier heights—along with Kansas gourmet products and apple-theme gifts, you'll also find KC barbecue goodies. Sauces like K&M, Jazzy's, Chef Dan's, and Buckaroo are on display, plus spices, herbs, rubs, and BBQ cookbooks to get you set up for some great backyard 'que. The store is open year-round, but hours are shorter in the wintertime. The apple doughnuts are a must taste!

MISSOURI MEMORIES

Seville Square, 500 Nichols Road, Kansas City, MO 64112; (816)931-9174

Several Kansas City barbecue sauces and spices are predominately displayed at this shop on the Country Club Plaza. Owner Nancy Welchon founded Missouri Memories in 1984, and she stocks a slew of giftables from the "Show Me State." This is also the place to let your sense of humor feast on lots of T-shirts and gift cards. A special pack of three barbecue sauces makes an easy take-home gift.

POOL & PATIO, INC.
11409 W. 89th Street, Overland Park, KS 66214; (913)888-2226

Lou Furlo's shop carries everything for the pool and patio. His choice of barbecue rigs is the Hasty Bake Oven. Several models are on display, and any of the units manufactured can be special ordered (including the top-of-the-line stainless steel model, which will last a lifetime). Hasty Bake accessories sold here include hardwood charcoal, rib racks, grill brushes, and grill covers to protect these superb smokers.

PRYDE'S OLD WESTPORT
115 Westport Road, Kansas City, MO 64111; (816)531-5588

Pryde's is a treasure trove for the serious cook, chock full of gourmet foods, utensils, tabletop items, wooden chopping blocks, and more. Pryde's barbecue fare is first rate. They stock over a dozen barbecue sauces, and the accessories take the cake—grill baskets for fish, chicken, or hamburgers, different-sized grill toppers, temperature gauges, skewers, mitts, aprons, picnic baskets, checkered tablecloths, long-handled tongs, spatulas, basting brushes, and mops.

SUMMIT OUTDOOR LIVING
606 N.E. 291 Highway, Lee's Summit, MO 64086; (816)246-8700

Located at the corner of Chipman Road and 291, this is "cowtown central" for lovers of the Oklahoma Joe line of smokers (nine models sit on the display room floor). Owners Nita and Gary Tripp show the large trailer unit on Saturdays in the parking lot beside the store. The resulting sweet-scented billowing barbecue cloud entices you to taste their treats and encourages you to buy this competition-sized cooker. The award-winning line of Oklahoma Joe's barbecue sauces and spices plus Lampson and Goodnow barbecue accessories also are available here.

★ WOODS ★

Most full-service groceries in the KC area sell hickory and mesquite wood chips, but wood chunks and logs are hard to find. The following sources stock many varieties of woods, and we encourage you to experiment to determine your favorite.

AMERICAN WOOD PRODUCTS
9540 Riggs, Overland Park, KS 66212; (913)648-7993

Here you can load up on mesquite, pecan, hickory, grape, oak, apple, cherry, and alder logs, slabs, chunks, and chips. Mesquite or hardwood lump charcoal also available. (Wholesale and retail.)

FAIRLANE FIREPLACE & BAR B Q WOOD
12520 3rd Street, Grandview, MO 64030; (816)761-1350

This place stocks apple, cherry, pecan, hickory, oak, sassafras, mesquite, maple, and grape woods, from dust to logs. (Wholesale and retail.)

★ CONTESTS ★

From April through October, there's a barbecue competition almost every weekend in the KC area. Most are held in conjunction with a community festival or charity event. Pitmasters set up on Friday and cook for friends and family, then prepare for competition on Saturday. Most cook-offs invite the public to visit, and it's a great way to visit with the chefs and pick up a few tips. Most are happy to share their award-winning techniques.

Most contests in this area are sanctioned by the Kansas City Barbeque Society (KCBS). For a complete listing of contests and dates, contact the KCBS, 11514 Hickman Mills Drive, Kansas City, MO 64134; (816)765-5891. The following is a sample of contests that are well established and encourage the public to attend.

JUNE

THE GREAT LENEXA BARBECUE BATTLE
Lenexa, KS

Held the last weekend in June, 160 teams compete here for the Kansas State Champion title. This community celebration and competition exemplifies why Lenexa is called the "Kansas Rising Star": it takes over 400 judges to sample the 960 entries. Contact: Lenexa Parks and Recreation, 13420 Oak Street, Lenexa, KS 66215; (913) 541-8592.

JULY

MIDWEST REGIONAL BARBEQUE CHAMPIONSHIP
Gladstone, MO

For this one, the weather's hot, the competition is keen, the park is shaded, and the hospitality is grand. The Friday night BBQ feed and street dance draws thousands. Contact: Gladstone Area Chamber of Commerce, P.O. Box 10751, Gladstone, MO, 64118; (816)436-4523.

SEPTEMBER

BLUE SPRINGS BLAZE-OFF
Blue Springs, MO

The weekend after Labor Day is the perfect time for this premier competition. Over 75 of the area's best teams turn out for the competition, parade, and festivities. Contact: Parks and Recreation, City of Blue Springs, 903 Main Street, Blue Springs, MO 64015; (816)228-0137.

OCTOBER

THE AMERICAN ROYAL BARBECUE CONTEST
Kansas City, MO

This "grand finale" of the barbecue season is the largest barbecue contest in the world. Consisting of several events (the American Royal/K.C. Masterpiece International Invitational Barbecue Contest, the American Royal Open Barbecue Contest, the Side Dish Contest, the Wings Contest, and the American Royal International Barbecue Sauce Contest), this is a "can't miss" affair. Continuous music, family entertainment, and world-class barbecue make for one fine weekend. Contact: Pam McKee, American Royal Association, 1701 American Royal Court, Kansas City, MO 64102; (816)221-9800.

★ ASSOCIATIONS AND INSTRUCTION ★

Learn more about the art of barbecue from professional associations, schools, and publications.

BARBECUE INDUSTRY ASSOCIATION
710 E. Ogden, Suite 113, Naperville, IL 60540; (708)369-2404

The membership of this association is geared to manufacturers of consumer barbecue goods. They provide lobbying, periodic consumer surveys, and research for the industry.

BARON'S BARBECUE SCHOOL
The Recipe Exchange, 3625 W. 50th Terrace, Roeland Park, KS 66205;
  (913)262-6029 (or contact the Kansas City Barbeque Society)

Chef Paul Kirk, C.W.C., Ph.B., S.B.S.A., gives intensive and detailed hands-on instruction at his classes. Learn the art of trimming and smoking meats; developing sauces, rubs, and marinades; and preparing and tending to the fire. Great barbecue skills are guaranteed!

COMMUNIVERSITY
University of Missouri–Kansas City
5100 Rockhill Road, Kansas City, MO 64110; (816)235-1448

Communiversity classes are offered periodically throughout the year. Look for Guy Simpson's (the KC Rib Doctor) class on barbecue. He reveals his techniques for smoking and grilling, dry rubs, marinades, and sauces.

HAPPY "HOLLA" CHAMPIONSHIP BARBECUE VIDEO
P.O. Box 822, Shawnee Mission, KS 66201; (913)268-7828

Nothing is held back here! Ed Roith shares his expertise for the competition barbecue cooking of ribs, poultry, pork, and brisket in this 90-minute video.

KANSAS CITY BARBEQUE SOCIETY
11514 Hickman Mills Drive, Kansas City, MO 64134; (816)765-5891

The largest organization of its kind, this group produces the *Bullsheet* newsletter and sanctions barbecue contests throughout the country. You can join for a modest annual dues fee.

NATIONAL BARBECUE ASSOCIATION
4401 Colwick Road, Suite 107, Charlotte, NC 28211; (704)365-3622

The NBBQA holds the only annual convention and trade show dedicated to the barbecue industry. Membership is comprised of backyard enthusiasts, manufacturers, restaurateurs, barbecue retailers, and related trade.

PIG OUT PUBLICATIONS, INC.
4245 Walnut Street, Kansas City, MO 64111; (816)531-3119

This is the largest publisher and distributor specializing solely in barbecue and grill books. Write or call for a catalog. Mail order welcome!

★ INDEX ★

★ ABOUT THE AUTHORS ★

Coauthor of two cookbooks and author of numerous articles on barbecue, Rich Davis has spent many years grillside, and the fruits of his labors have helped to make Kansas City barbecue a nationally recognized culinary treasure. His father built stone wood-burning grills and smokers, fascinating him at a very young age with the techniques of building fires and grilling steaks and burgers. By his early adult years Rich had become a serious barbecue aficionado (as well as a family and child psychiatrist).

Amateur barbecuers in the 1940s and '50s nearly always created their own barbecue sauce, and Rich Davis was no exception. A friend's simple five-ingredient recipe spurred him on to the dozen-or-so-ingredient version that America knows today as K.C. Masterpiece. That homemade sauce won first place in the very first American Royal Barbecue Contest. And later became the tasty reason he was called to do the barbecue for the movie Murphy's Romance, and invited to barbecue for the president on the White House lawn, and then to join with Wolfgang Puck, Jeremiah Tower, Jonathon Waxman, and other renowned chefs in putting on a James Beard charity barbecue at Rockefeller Center. K.C. Masterpiece has become a popular national brand—the No. 1 seller in the premium category of barbecue sauces reports the Clorox Company, which purchased the label in 1986.

Rich's lifelong love affair with "Kansas City–style" barbecue hasn't stopped with his taste for sauce. That passion also has led, with his sons, to the growing operations of the K.C. Masterpiece BBQ & Grill restaurants—there are two now in Kansas City, two in St. Louis, and two in the Chicago suburbs of Downers Grove and Buffalo Grove.

With nearly 20 books to her credit, author and publisher Shifra Stein is the creator of the acclaimed *Day Trips®* series for Kansas City, Nashville, San Antonio–Austin, and other major metropolitan areas. She has authored numerous guides to Kansas City, among them *A Kid's Guide To Kansas City* and *Kansas City Guide,* and coauthored *The All-American Barbecue Book* (also with Rich Davis), *Kansas City Cuisine,* and *Heart of America: Kansas City.* An award-winning food and travel journalist, she is the former restaurant critic for *The Kansas City Star* and previously hosted a syndicated food and travel segment aired nationally on 150 stations on the WAXWORKS Radio Network.
Shifra is a member of the Society of American Travel Writers and recipient of a fellowship from the University of Missouri–Kansas City's Greater Kansas City Writing Project. She currently offers life-changing journaling workshops

and journaling seminars in conjunction with area counseling organizations, schools, and churches. A well-known speaker, she also provides a variety of presentations for groups, including "Day Trips," "Great Romantic Getaways," and "Travel Safety on the Road." For more information on Shifra Stein Seminars, call (913)262-9456.

Order Form

ORDER DIRECT—(816) 531-3119 OR FAX (816) 531-6113

YES! I want some barbecue cookbooks so I can start cooking like the pros! Please send me:

___copy(s) **ALL ABOUT BAR-B-QUE KANSAS CITY–STYLE** for $14.95
___copy(s) **BARBECUE GREATS MEMPHIS–STYLE** for $14.95
___copy(s) **BAR-B-QUE, BARBECUE, BARBEQUE, BAR-B-Q, B-B-Q** for $5.95
___copy(s) **BARBECUING & SAUSAGE-MAKING SECRETS** for $14.95
___copy(s) **HOOKED ON FISH ON THE GRILL** for $9.95
___copy(s) **THE PASSION OF BARBEQUE** for $9.95
___copy(s) **TEXAS BARBECUE** for $14.95

Shipping and handling added as follows:
    1 book = $3.75, 2 books = $4.75, 3–5 books = $6.00
___Please put me on the mailing list!

METHOD OF PAYMENT

___Enclosed is my check for $_____ (payable to Pig Out Publications, Inc.)
___Please charge to my credit card: __VISA __MasterCard

Acct.# _____Exp. date _____

Signature _____

SHIP TO: _____   **GIFT/SHIP TO:** _____

_____   _____

_____   _____

_____   _____

_____   _____

SEND COMPLETED ORDER FORM TO:
Pig Out Publications, Inc. • 4245 Walnut Street • Kansas City, MO 64111